The Making of the 20th Century

This series of specially commissioned titles focuses attention on significant and often controversial events and themes of world history in the present century. Each book provides sufficient narrative and explanation for the newcomer to the subject while offering, for more advanced study, detailed source-references and bibliographies, together with interpretation and reassessment in the light of recent scholarship.

In the choice of subjects there is a balance between breadth in some spheres and detail in others; between the essentially political and matters economic or social. The series cannot be a comprehensive account of everything that has happened in the twentieth century, but it provides a guide to recent research and explains something of the times of extraordinary change and complexity in which we live. It is directed in the main to students of contemporary history and international relations, but includes titles which are of direct relevance to courses in economics, sociology, politics and geography.

The Making of the 20th Century

The Rise of the International Organisation: A Short History

David Armstrong

MACMILLAN

First published 1982
Reprinted 1988, 1990

Published by
MACMILLAN EDUCATION LTD
Houndmills, Basingstoke, Hampshire RG21 2XS
and London
Companies and representatives
throughout the world

Printed in Hong Kong

ISBN 0–333–27485–7 (paperback)

Contents

Preface

The proliferation of international organisations in this century has been accompanied by a mountain of documents and a vast array of secondary literature. The latter has been marked by a growing theoretical sophistication but also, in the case of general texts, by ever-increasing length as authors have tried to do justice to the diversity and complexity of international institutions. This has made the study of international organisation seem a somewhat daunting task to students new to the subject, and I offer this book as a modest effort in overcoming this problem. I have tried to provide a short historical overview of the subject which is more than just a long list of names, dates and functions, but which does not lose sight of the need in some cases for factual detail or analytical depth.

An inevitable problem with a work of this kind is that it must omit much and treat many important topics with a brevity they do not always deserve. In the end, like any other author, I have relied primarily on my own personal preferences and interests to guide me in the selection of material to include in this book. There is no single theme running through it, although there is an underlying assumption that international organisations are, first and foremost, the creatures and instruments of states. Hence, there is less in this study than in some others on the role of international secretariats and perhaps rather more on the varied motivations of states in their approach to international organisations. Similarly, certain events are considered in relatively more detail than others, such as the Abyssinian crisis of 1935 or the EEC's constitutional crisis of 1965. This, too, reflects the general emphasis on states, since both cases involved a fundamental collision between the larger aspirations of international organisations and the constraints imposed upon them by the imperatives of the state system within which they operate.

This book is based on the historical section of the international organisation course which I give at Birmingham University, and I should like to take this opportunity to thank past and present students for their many helpful comments. I am also indebted to my colleagues in Birmingham's School of International Studies, the Head of the School, David Wightman, and Jon Haslam and John Redmond, for freely dispensing of their time and expertise, although I naturally accept full responsibility for any errors of fact or judgement. I am also grateful to my publishers, especially Sarah Mahaffy, and the general editor of the series, Geoffrey Warner, for their patience and support. Most of all my thanks go to Maggie, Celyn and Iain for more than I can express here.

3 November 1981   J. D. ARMSTRONG
Birmingham

Abbreviations

ACP	African, Caribbean and Pacific region
ASA	Association of South-east Asia
ASEAN	Association of South-east Asian Nations
CACM	Central American Common Market
CAP	Common Agricultural Policy
COREPER	Committee of Permanent Representatives
EAGGF	European Agricultural Guidance and Guarantee Fund
ECAFE	Economic Commission for Asia and the Far East
ECOSOC	Economic and Social Council
ECOWAS	Economic Community of West African States
ECSC	European Coal and Steel Community
EDC	European Defence Community
EEC	European Economic Community
EEZ	Exclusive Economic Zone
EFTA	European Free Trade Association
EMS	European Monetary System
EURATOM	European Atomic Energy Community
FAO	Food and Agriculture Organisation
GATT	General Agreement on Tariff and Trade
ICAO	International Civil Aviation Organisation
IICI	International Institute for Intellectual Co-operation
ILO	International Labour Organisation
IMF	International Monetary Fund
LAFTA	Latin American Free Trade Association
MLF	Multilateral Nuclear Force
NIEO	New International Economic Order
OAS	Organisation of American States
OAU	Organisation of African Unity
ODECA	Organisation of Central American States
OECD	Organisation for Economic Co-operation and Development
OEEC	Organisation of European Economic Co-operation
ONUC	Operation des Nations Unies au Congo
OPEC	Organisation of Petroleum Exporting Countries
SEATO	South-east Asia Treaty Organisation

SELA   Latin American Economic System
UNCLOS   United Nations Conference on the Law of the Sea
UNCTAD   United Nations Conference on Trade and Development
UNDP   United Nations Development Programme
UNEF   United Nations Emergency Force
UNESCO   United Nations Educational, Scientific and Cultural
            Organisation
UNFICYP   United Nations Force in Cyprus
UNHCR   United Nations Office of the High Commissioner for
            Refugees
UNICEF   United Nations Children's Fund
UNIDO   United Nations Industrial Development Organisation
UNIFIL   United Nations Force in Lebanon
UNMOGIP   United Nations Military Observer Group for India and
            Pakistan
UNOGIL   United Nations Observer Group in Lebanon
UNSCOB   United Nations Special Committee on the Balkans
UNSCOP   United Nations Special Committee on Palestine
UNYOM   United Nations Yemen Observation Mission
WHO   World Health Organisation

1 The Origins of the League of Nations

The creation of the League of Nations was an extraordinary event. Not only had there been nothing like it before, but there was very little in the system of international relations which existed in 1914 or in the previous history of diplomacy to suggest its possibility. The guiding principle of all states in their relations with each other was the protection of their national sovereignty, and any development that might interfere with this, even in a very small way, had always been resisted. International co-operation in the most important area of peace and security had, perhaps inevitably, been limited and temporary, but even in much less contentious matters, such as setting up an efficient international postal system, or deciding upon rules to govern the laying down of marine cables, or regulating the spread of epidemic diseases by international sanitary conventions, progress had taken many years. In each case this was because one or more states had opposed change in the belief that its sovereignty might be infringed or that it might lose some narrow national advantage. Even so derisory an issue as an attempt to determine internationally agreed safety standards in the manufacture of matches had been vigorously resisted by Britain on the latter grounds. Yet a few years after this episode Britain was one of the principal founders of the League: a permanent international organisation with wide-ranging responsibilities.

The League, therefore, was not simply the culmination of a long evolutionary process but was also in some respects a radical departure from past practice, owing as much to the immediate circumstances of its creation as to the previous history of international organisation. This chapter is devoted to a detailed discussion of the origins of the League but for the sake of clarity it will be useful first to consider briefly the relative importance of the various factors which contributed something to the League's genesis.

In certain limited respects the League may be seen as the logical outcome of developments in international co-operation in the nineteenth century. After the defeat of Napoleon in 1815 the European powers had formed the habit of consulting regularly with each other in the system known as the Concert of Europe. The Concert system also signified an acceptance of the principle that the great powers had some special responsibility for the management of international affairs and the maintenance of international order. Secondly, the enormous growth in the quantity and range of interaction between states in the nineteenth century created a correspondingly greater need for some regulation of those relations or in other words for a more developed international legal system. States increasingly resorted to legal or quasi-legal means of resolving their minor disputes and the nineteenth century witnessed a notable growth in the practice of submitting such disputes to arbitration tribunals. In some cases permanent international institutions were established to regulate certain areas of international life. Two of the primary purposes of the League were to give international law a more central role in international relations and to institutionalise the Concert of Europe's principles of great power consultation and collective responsibility for international order, so to that extent there were important antecedents to the League in the nineteenth century. But some more immediate considerations were of at least equal significance.

The first of these was the impact of the 1914–18 war. This gave rise to a widespread discontent with international relations in their present form and to demands for a new collective security system which would outlaw aggression. When the American President, Woodrow Wilson, publicly supported the general principle of reforming the international system in May 1916, he lent credibility to the various unofficial schemes for a League of Nations which meant that the major European states were obliged to take the idea more seriously. The Russian revolution of 1917 provided an additional reason for the European powers to seek to change the international order since this was the most appropriate means of countering the adverse propaganda effects of the Bolshevik demands for an end to the old diplomacy. Draft constitutions for a League of Nations appeared from several official quarters during 1918, with discussions during the peace conference of 1919 based on a joint Anglo-American draft.

But the League also had many important features whose true origin is to be discovered in the period of intensive inter-allied diplomacy just before and during the peace conference: diplomacy that was guided in the main by a variety of short-term considerations. This meant that the League which was eventually decided was not in all respects a carefully constructed edifice, built upon past experience and the outcome of orderly deliberations. Winston Churchill wrote of the Paris Peace Conference as a whole: 'Decisions were taken not as the result of systematised study and discussion but only when some individual topic reached a condition of crisis. Throughout there was no considered order of priority, no thought-out plan of descending from the general to the particular'.[1] It could hardly be expected that the meetings of the

League of Nations Commission, which drafted the Covenant of the League, alone remained immune from the effects of this atmosphere.

THE DEVELOPMENT OF INTERNATIONAL ORGANISATIONS BEFORE 1919

The profound changes in the political, economic and social landscape during the nineteenth and early twentieth centuries were instrumental both in establishing a favourable climate for the proliferation of international organisations and in determining their agenda. This is most obvious in the fields of trade and international communications. The massive increase in production sparked off by the Industrial Revolution led to an equally heavy growth in trade; with the coming of steam this trade was carried on at ever-faster rates on land and sea. As more and more of the globe was penetrated by European imperialism, so a highly complex worldwide economic network emerged. This influenced the growth of international institutions in four distinct ways. Firstly, the greater number of international transactions increased the risk of war arising out of some trivial conflict. This was one factor behind the growing tendency during the nineteenth century for states to accept international arbitration of various types of disputes where, as the standard formula ran, 'neither honour nor vital interests' were involved.[2] Secondly, agreed regulations and common standards had to be determined for such purposes as patenting inventions, classifying goods for customs duties and deciding exchange rates between currencies. What were then termed 'public international unions' were established to deal with such matters, and by the end of the nineteenth century the movement towards international standardisation had begun in less technical and more obviously political fields, such as the protection of workers and children. Thirdly, the traditional insistence by states upon a rigid interpretation of their sovereign rights became an increasingly serious barrier to the efficient conduct of international business. The classic illustration of this concerned the transmission of postal items across frontiers. Before the establishment of the General Postal Union in 1875 and its successor, the Universal Postal Union in 1878, international postal communication was governed by numerous bilateral treaties rather than by a single convention. The objective of each state was to ensure that the balance of financial advantage deriving from these treaties was in its favour, which led to extremely high foreign postage rates being charged by all. As charges were levied at each frontier, the cost of sending a postal item from one country to another varied according to the route taken, with a ½ oz. letter from the United States to Australia costing anything from five cents to $1.02.[3] Fourthly, the economies of the major powers were becoming increasingly interdependent, which provided them with certain mutual interests to set against their many rivalries.[4] The nineteenth century saw the first attempts to translate this interdependence into institutional form through the establishment of international commissions to regulate the trade of specific commodities, such as sugar.[5] Another effect of interdependence was that it helped to internationalise issues – to turn what would once have been purely national questions into matters of general concern. The control of disease was one such area, in which several international unions had been set up by the end of the century. The first of these, in 1838, was the Conseil Supérieur de Santé at Constantinople, whose aim was to prevent the introduction of cholera into Turkey. This was followed by sanitary councils in Tangier, Teheran, Alexandria and elsewhere and eventually by the important Sanitary Convention of 1903 and the establishment of the International Office of Public Hygiene in 1907.[6]

None of these landmarks in the history of international organisation had an untroubled birth, nor did they hint at any prospect of more ambitious undertakings being successful. France, fearing possible financial losses, had delayed the formation of the postal union; Britain had resisted for many years any attempt to sign a sanitary convention on the grounds that this might harm her maritime interests. The sanitary councils had themselves been arenas for the conflicts of great power interests that went on throughout the nineteenth century.

The continuing influence of national rivalries may be illustrated further by two of the most acclaimed events of the turn of the century: the Hague Conferences of 1899 and 1907. These originated from a proposal for a disarmament conference made by Tsar Nicholas II and marked the high point in the history of international arbitration. They were also the most widely attended conferences to date, with delegates from Europe, North and South America and Asia, their popularity being a clear response to the interdependence that many now felt to be a crucial factor in international relations. As the President of the first Conference put it: 'We perceive that there is a community of material and moral interests between nations, which is constantly increasing . . . . If a nation wished to remain isolated it could not . . . It is part of a single organism.'[7] The most important implication of this interdependence was, he felt, that 'when a dispute arises between two or more nations, the others, without being directly involved, are seriously affected'. This in turn meant that further machinery for states to submit their disputes for mediation, conciliation or arbitration needed to be developed.[8]

Although many delegates echoed these sentiments, they found it more difficult to agree upon the concrete obligations their states would have to accept if these principles were to be given substance. The discussions at the Hague Conferences consisted of a curious amalgam of idealistic statements of purpose and careful disavowals by everyone that they were undertaking any binding commitments. Hence the specific achievements of the first Conference were few: a so-called Permanent Court of Arbitration[9] and some provision for the use of International Commissions of Inquiry in certain disputes. The second Conference revised the conventions that had been agreed by the first and added ten new ones. Somewhat ominously these mostly concerned the laws of war. No significant progress was made in the area of disarmament – the original occasion of the Conferences.

The Hague agreements were hailed at the time as a new beginning in international relations but they achieved little, and when the League of Nations was being constructed at the Paris Peace Conference, the Hague experience was generally ignored. Concerned about this, Léon Bourgeois, the French delegate to the Paris Commission responsible for drafting the Covenant, who had played a notable part at The Hague, made several attempts to link the Covenant to the work of the Hague Conferences. In this he was supported only by the Portuguese delegate, who made a formal declaration regretting that the League of Nations Commission was not attempting to advance the work of the Hague Conferences in arbitration. All such pressure was resisted by the British and Americans, who argued that the League needed to be free from any association with previous ventures.[10] The only concession made in the Covenant to the sensibilities of Léon Bourgeois was what has been described as an 'afterthought' in the form of a reference in Article 13 stating that certain disputes might be suitable for arbitration.[11]

The only nineteenth-century international institution to have a directly important influence on the League of Nations Covenant was the Concert of Europe: the informal arrangement whereby the European powers consulted together at times of crisis. The Concert, originating in the post-Napoleonic settlement, had at first fluctuated between the opposing concepts of the Tsar and Metternich, on the one hand, that the Concert should be a kind of international government with wide powers of intervention in the domestic affairs of states, and Castlereagh and Canning, on the other hand, who upheld 'all correct notions of internal sovereign authority'.[12] Later it settled down into a loose association of major powers with the primary aim of preventing the Eastern Question from getting out of hand and with a general concern to uphold international order when this did not conflict unduly with their separate national interests. In the forty years up to 1914 the Concert system decreased in significance until its last meeting to consider the Albanian situation in 1913, when, in the opinion of one of the participants, it still had a useful, albeit very modest role to play:

We had not settled anything, not even all the details of the Albanian boundaries; but we had served a useful purpose. We had been something to which point after point could be referred; we had been a means of keeping all the six powers in direct and friendly contact. The mere fact that we were in existence and that we should have to be broken up before peace was broken, was in itself an appreciable barrier against war. We were a means of gaining time, and the longer we remained in being the more reluctance was there for us to disperse. The Governments concerned got used to us and to the habit of making us useful.[13]

Considerations of this kind played a part in the deliberations at the Paris Peace Conference, while the underlying idea of the Concert – that the great powers possessed distinctive rights and duties with regard to the management of international relations – was embodied in the League Council, which was seen, at least by the great powers, as an institutionalised Concert.

However the League probably owed less to the Concert itself than it did to the breakdown of the balance of power which had underpinned the Concert until the emergence of modern Germany. This, together with the rise to world power of a United States which had long distrusted traditional European diplomacy, and with the new social pressures that had been building up during the nineteenth century and which culminated in the Russian Revolution, contributed significantly to the political climate in Paris in 1919.

THE LEAGUE IDEA AND THE ROLE OF WOODROW WILSON

Schemes to replace the endemic anarchy of international relations by a system designed to ensure peace, security and order were not unique to this century, but the unparalleled destruction of the First World War meant that for the first time they had to be taken seriously by the practitioners as well as the theorists of politics. Not only was there a popular clamour for some new means of controlling international violence which democratically elected statesmen could hardly ignore, but the old international order had been decisively swept away, and its only successors with clear-cut answers to everything were Lenin's Bolsheviks, who threatened to overthrow the domestic orders as well. The Western powers at Paris were well aware of this, and the first problem that faced them was how to translate into concrete form a bewildering range of ideas as to what the League should be, while ensuring that the resulting organisation offered a viable reformist alternative to the revolutionary vision of the Bolsheviks.

The term 'League of Nations' probably originated with Léon Bourgeois's book, *La Société des Nations*, published in 1908.[14] Bourgeois was one of a number of leading figures from several countries who, having advocated a new system for the management of international relations before the war, became active in popular movements to that end during it. In the United States these included two former Presidents, Roosevelt and Taft, who called for what would today be termed a collective security system: some arrangement whereby aggressors would incur automatic economic and military sanctions imposed by the whole international community.[15] Taft was one of the sponsors in June 1915 of the League to Enforce Peace, a pressure group with the objective of promoting a League of Nations based on the twin principles of collective security and a greatly enhanced status for international law.[16] Similar groups existed in Britain, France and elsewhere, most of them basing their programmes on an extension of the work of the Hague Conferences in the field of arbitration.[17]

The impact of these groups was strictly limited. They helped to focus public opinion upon the idea of a new international order and they popularised the name 'League of Nations', but the League that was eventually created owed little of substance to their efforts. The first detailed British government draft of a possible League, the Phillimore Report, accepted some of their underlying ideas but dismissed as 'impracticable' their specific provisions.[18] Similar sentiments were more forcefully expressed by such hardened realists as Lloyd George and Clemenceau. More significantly, President Woodrow Wilson, regarded by many as the 'father' of the League, refused to associate himself with any of the unofficial schemes, privately referring to the members of organisations like the League to Enforce Peace as 'woolgatherers'.[19]

Wilson's role in the genesis of the League is a complex one which needs elucidating in some detail. It is clear that he was convinced from an early stage that a new international system was required and that he saw in this the means of obtaining both personal glory and power and prestige for his country. Later, in common with other statesmen, he came to pin a variety of additional aspirations upon the League, including resisting the Bolshevik threat, underwriting the peace treaties, democratising the world, establishing a new economic order (with a pre-eminent role for the United States) and ending the colonial system. However he had few, if any, well-defined ideas as to the actual form of the new organisation which was to bring about this diplomatic revolution.

Even before the war, Wilson had shown some interest in novel means of securing peace. His first Secretary of State, Bryan, had promoted a series of bilateral treaties whose principal feature was an agreement that, should a dispute arise, the states involved would observe a moratorium of one year to permit investigation and attempts at arbitration before resorting to war.[20] This unlikely notion that a 'cooling-off' period might lower temperatures sufficiently to prevent war was to reappear as Article 12 of the Covenant. A more significant early influence was an abortive attempt by Wilson and his close adviser, Colonel House, to sponsor a Pan-American Treaty in which an important element would be an article committing all parties to 'a common and mutual guarantee of territorial integrity and of political independence under republican forms of government'.[21] A similar wording was to be used in the last of Wilson's famous Fourteen Points on the peace settlement in January 1918.[22] House later claimed that he had all along seen this treaty as a model for a future European settlement.[23] Significantly, in November 1918, when the Director of the Inquiry (Wilson's group of researchers and advisers on the peace settlement) was searching for relevant information, he asked Secretary of State Lansing for a copy of the treaty, offering revealingly to 'use it as a possible form of general international agreement without indicating that it was in contemplation an agreement for this hemisphere'.[24]

The idea of mutual guarantees of independence and territorial integrity appeared in Wilson's first public endorsement of the concept of a League of Nations on 27 May 1916, when he advocated

a universal association of the nations to maintain the inviolate security of the highway of the seas for the common good and unhindered use of all the nations of the world, and to prevent any war begun either contrary to treaty covenants or without warning and full submission of the causes to the opinion of the world — a virtual guarantee of territorial integrity and political independence.[25]

The reference here to a possible League role in maintaining freedom of the seas was not likely to gain the support of the British government, given its traditional insistence upon naval hegemony. Anglo-American clashes over the purpose of the League were also foreshadowed in an Inquiry memorandum in December 1917, which called for a League 'for the attainment of a joint economic prosperity including equal opportunity upon the highways of the world and equitable access to the raw materials which all nations need'.[26]

Wilson's notion of mutual guarantees had much in common with the collective security principle, as did a later comment that the old-style balance of power needed to be replaced by a 'community of power'.[27] However, Wilson had gone over his May 1916 speech shortly before delivering it and erased any reference to the possible use of physical force against transgressors, thus stopping short of endorsing the fundamental prerequisite of a collective security system.[28] This reflected his reluctance to go beyond high-sounding generalisations to any specific formula for a League of Nations. The reasons for this reluctance, which persisted right up to 1919, are complex. Firstly, he was justifiably afraid that the Senate might refuse to ratify any treaty which appeared to commit American troops to upholding the New Diplomacy.[29] Secondly, he was particularly unwilling to make public any detailed project for a League on the grounds that this would stir up controversy. This was why he frequently resisted pressure to reveal his own ideas for a League both from unofficial League enthusiasts and also from House, who was anxious that public discussion should crystallise around Wilson's plan for a League rather than someone else's.[30] Thirdly, one of the few consistent elements in Wilson's approach to the League from 1916 to 1919 was his insistence that it needed to be an organic 'living thing', that the 'administrative constitution of the League must grow and not be made; that we must begin with solemn covenants covering mutual guarantees of political independence and territorial integrity . . . but that the method of carrying those mutual pledges out should be left to develop of itself, case by case'.[31]

It was also true, however, that while Wilson brushed aside most designs for a League that emanated from private or allied sources – or even from his Secretary of State, Lansing – his own thinking on the League displayed considerable uncertainty and confusion. Most British schemes for a League revolved around the idea of an institutionalised great power Concert, and the first draft constitution of a League offered to Wilson by Colonel House in July 1918 had similarly excluded smaller powers. Wilson rejected this proposal that the League should be a great power club but continued to insist that it should be 'virile' without seeming to appreciate that the presence of small states could be a source of impotence.[32] Precisely what was to be the foundation of this virility was never made clear by Wilson. Moreover any definite ideas he might once have had as to the purpose of the League had become so diluted by 1919 that it is hardly surprising that so many conflicting and unrealistic expectations came to be attached to the League by less eminent observers.

Sometimes Wilson spoke as if the League's peacekeeping objective was to be achieved mainly by open diplomacy and the pressure of public opinion:

My conception of the League of Nations is just this, that it shall operate as the organised moral force of men throughout the world and that whenever or wherever wrong and aggression are planned or contemplated, this searching light of conscience will be turned upon them and men everywhere will ask, 'What are the purposes that you hold in your heart against the fortunes of the world?' Just a little exposure will settle most questions. If the Central Powers had dared to discuss the purposes of this war for a single fortnight, it never would have happened.[33]

On other occasions his original emphasis on mutual guarantees (which was reiterated in Article 10 of the Covenant) was claimed to be the 'backbone' of the League, without which it 'could hardly be more than an influential debating society'.[34] He could still, however, claim to the American Senate that Article 10 was 'binding in conscience only, not in law', and just before the Peace Conference had said privately that he expected economic sanctions to be the main weapon to be used against aggressors.[35]

Wilson also indulged in the tendency in common with others so widespread during the last six months of 1918 to graft on to the League additional functions which diminished its fundamental security role. One such instance was the responsibility undertaken by the League in its 'mandates' system for the former enemy colonies. The fifth of Wilson's Fourteen Points had called for an adjustment of colonial claims, taking into account the interests of the populations. When House attempted to interpret this point to the United States' allies during his mission to Europe in October 1918, he took it a stage further: 'It would seem as if the principle involved in this proposition is that a colonial power acts not as owner of its colonies but as a trustee for the natives and for the society of nations.'[36] A British Foreign Office memorandum in November suggested that certain colonial areas might be administered by individual powers under a League of Nations mandate.[37] As late as 10 December Wilson, in discussion with his Inquiry team, believed that it was possible for the German colonies to become the common property of the League and be administered by the smaller nations.[38] However, when General Smuts published his detailed plan for a League, Wilson enthusiastically endorsed his basic idea of a mandates system, although Smuts excluded from this the former German colonies in the Pacific and Africa as being 'inhabited by barbarians', whereas Wilson was to argue at Paris that they too should be amongst the League's mandated territories.[39] By the time of the Peace Conference the mandates question, which had started life as a peripheral issue, had become so important to Wilson that he could maintain in his arguments with the other major powers that the League 'would be a laughing stock if it were not invested with this quality of trusteeship'.[40]

Wilson's lack of a clear and comprehensive blueprint for a League, together with his evasiveness on the issue, were such that as late as 6 January 1919 the chief British Cabinet supporter of the League, Lord Robert Cecil, had 'little idea of what the President's conception of a League really involved'.[41] None the less the popular depiction of Wilson as 'father of the League' has some validity. His chief contribution, however, was not so much as the originator of the Covenant[42] but rather lay in his insistence throughout 1918 that some edifice bearing the title 'League of Nations' should be created, that the League should be the first item on the Paris agenda and that it should be an integral part of the peace treaty.[43]

THE DRAFTING OF THE COVENANT

Part of Wilson's problem was that he had come to distrust his own State Department and in particular his Secretary of State, Robert Lansing, whom he considered to be too cautious and legalistic in his approach to the League.[44] Lansing differed from the President firstly in the importance each attached to the League — Lansing insisted that the prime necessity was to push for the democratisation of authoritarian countries[45] — and secondly in his conception of the League. Whereas Wilson's thinking, vague though it was, entailed a *positive* commitment by all League members to employ sanctions against aggressors, Lansing proposed a strengthening of existing diplomatic devices, such as arbitration and commissions of inquiry, but only a *negative* commitment by the powers to refrain from the use of violence in settling their disputes.[46] The result of the growing acrimony between the two was that Wilson refused to consider any analyses of the League idea that emanated from the State Department. Hence, at the start of 1919 all that Wilson had at his disposal in the way of detailed guidance on the League was a brief draft covenant drawn up by House in July 1918 and an equally short revision of this which Wilson himself had produced.[47] House's version was full of resonant phrases about 'honourable' and 'dishonourable' international behaviour and, while Wilson had avoided this temptation, his draft suffered from his inability to translate his ideas into precise terminology that could not be torn into shreds by the legal advisers of other governments. Despite the disdain felt by most of the British Cabinet towards the League idea, considerably more thought had been given in official British circles to its concrete implications, and several covenants existed by 1919, of which Smuts's was the most detailed. The French and Italians had also produced their own versions of the League by then.

The underlying principles and assumptions about the nature of the new international order, as they emerge from these documents, may be summarised as follows.

1 *Collective Security*

Although this term was not used until much later, its central theme — deterring potential aggressors by agreeing in advance to oppose them with a united front of all other states — was present in all of the deliberations of 1918–19. The collective security idea had been discussed in earlier international conferences, such as those after the Napoleonic wars, but its immediate origin lay in the belief that the First World War would have been prevented had Germany been aware beforehand of how extensive the opposition to it would become.

However, there were vast differences amongst the allies as to what a collective security system entailed in practice. The French, once they had become convinced of Wilson's determination to make the League the cornerstone of the entire settlement, pressed strongly for an international army to be created under a permanent general staff. The Wilson and House drafts placed most of their emphasis on the employment of an economic blockade – the weapon that had been effectively used during the war. Smuts, on the other hand, argued that economic sanctions alone would not be sufficient to deter a powerful state unless, as a last resort, they were backed by military force, but he was unwilling to go as far as the French in this direction. There were also voices raised against the whole concept of collective security. As early as May 1916 Sir Maurice Hankey, Secretary to the War Committee in Britain, argued strongly that the promise of security held out by such projects was 'wholly fictitious' and likely to foster dangerous illusions, especially in Britain.[48]

2   Justiciable Disputes

A common assumption in most drafts was that there was a clear distinction between international conflicts where a legal solution was possible and those where it was not. The former were defined by Smuts in this way:

Justiciable disputes are those which concern matters of fact or law which are capable of a legal or judicial handling. They involve mostly the interpretation of treaties or some other question of international law; or questions of fact, such as the situation of boundaries, or the amount of damage done by any breach of the law.[49]

It was widely believed that an extension of the existing legal remedies, such as arbitration, could take place under the auspices of the League, and Wilson and Smuts both proposed compulsory arbitration systems to that end. The Phillimore Report, while accepting arbitration in certain circumstances, laid greater stress on the use of conferences of major powers in the event of crisis, and this was to be a consistent element in all later British proposals. The final British draft of 20 January 1919, which was a synthesis of several earlier proposals, including a draft submitted by Lord Robert Cecil, did, however, call for a permanent international court to be established.[50]

3   Crisis Management

Understandably enough, most draft covenants were not really designed to prevent all conceivable wars but rather looked back to the origins of

the one which had just ended. This was seen by some to have developed
from a relatively minor crisis through a series of stages until it was out
of control. Hence there were several proposals for some means of
interrupting this relentless process of escalation. Suggestions included
compulsory moratoria while peaceful means of settling disputes could
be tried, as well as public discussions of the matters in dispute, since
Wilson believed that the secrecy of traditional diplomacy had been
partly to blame for the war.

4   Disarmament

A related set of proposals derived from the view that the arms race
before the war had helped to heighten international tension and that
the League, therefore, needed to develop some system of arms control.
This was to become an abiding concern of international organisations,
albeit one fraught with enormous difficulties. Schemes advanced in
1919 ranged from that of the French, who were chiefly interested in
ensuring German disarmament, to the British, who were mainly concerned with achieving the abolition of conscription, and the Americans,
who wanted a general arms-limitation agreement, including the abolition
of the private manufacture of weapons.

5   A Great Power Concert

A persistent theme of several members of the British Cabinet, as well as
of the Foreign Office, was that the only realistic means of bringing
more stability into international relations was to build upon the
practice of great power consultation that had developed during the
nineteenth century. One line of thought favoured the continuation in
peacetime of a body like the Supreme War Council, which would have
meant setting up the equivalent of a great power directorate of international affairs. An ambitious variant of this approach, proposed by the
British government in October 1918, called for joint allied control of
postwar economic reconstruction. This, however, was vetoed by the
Americans, who felt with some justice that such a scheme would entail
allied control of food and raw materials, which would inevitably be
provided mainly by the United States.[51] Less radical ideas involved an
institutionalised Concert of Europe, with either an arrangement for
continuous consultation amongst the powers or an agreement amongst
them to confer together at times of crisis. The common feature in all
such proposals was that they excluded smaller states from any significant role.

6   Functionalism

The approach to international organisation known as 'functionalism' holds that political integration amongst states can best develop from more limited attempts at co-operation in specific functional areas — principally those relating to economic welfare. Although functionalism as a systematic theoretical framework did not emerge until the work of David Mitrany in the 1930s and 1940s,[52] its central argument was advanced by Smuts in his 1918 pamphlet:

An attempt will be made in this sketch to give an essential extension to the functions of the League; indeed to look upon the League from a very different point of view, to view it not only as a possible means for preventing future wars, but much more as a great organ of the ordinary peaceful life of civilization, as the foundation of the new international system which will be erected on the ruins of this war and as the starting point from which the peace arrangements of the forthcoming conference should be made. Such an orientation of the idea seems to me necessary if the League is to become a permanent part of our international machinery. It is not sufficient for the League merely to be a sort of *deus ex machina*, called in in very grave emergencies when the spectre of war appears; if it is to last, it must be much more. It must become part and parcel of the common international life of states, it must be an ever visible, living, working organ of the polity of civilization.[53]

The idea that the League should not simply concern itself with security matters but should embrace a wide variety of additional functions (including some taken over from existing institutions) did not appear in Wilson's first draft of the Covenant, nor in the Phillimore or House proposals, and it was not fully developed in Smuts's paper. However, it gained momentum in the weeks before the Conference and during the actual Paris debates. One particular suggestion that was taken up by Wilson and others in this period was that the League should be involved in the development of international standards to apply to labour conditions.[54]

7   Organisational Principles

There was widespread agreement by the end of 1918 that the chief organs of the League should be an executive council, a deliberative assembly and an administrative secretariat, but considerable differences still existed as to the constitution and functions of each of these. The British, including their strongest supporter of the League, Lord Robert Cecil, wanted a Council of great powers only, with the other states confined to a very clearly subordinate role. Colonel House also favoured excluding the small states, but President Wilson was not willing to countenance this. Smuts and the Italian delegation independently suggested the novel device of having both permanent great power and non-permanent small power members of the Council, and this won Wilson's approval, appearing in his second attempt at a draft covenant, dated 10 January 1919.[55] However, the draft Covenant that was actually presented to the first session of the Paris Commission on the League on 3 February restricted places on the Council to the great powers, together with any smaller states they cared to invite — making small power membership an occasional privilege rather than a right. It was to take a great deal of pressure from the small nations before the powers accepted the Smuts–Italian formula.

Likewise, the nature and composition of the Assembly were far from settled as the delegates came together in Paris. The eventual role of the Assembly, which provided the model for the United Nations General Assembly, evolved in the years after the Conference, rather than being finally decided at Paris. In 1919 the British saw the Assembly as a talking shop that would meet very infrequently and would be composed either of parliamentarians or of representatives of the public. This was in line with earlier notions that the League should provide a forum for what Wilson had termed the 'organised opinion of mankind'. During one of the meetings of the Commission on the League in February, Cecil inadvertently revealed his country's view of the true status of the Assembly when he declared that England would probably 'send a leader of the Labour Party, someone who would be the spokesman of religious interests and, he hoped, a woman'.[56] For others, such as the Italians, the Assembly was to be taken more seriously and given powers to formulate and develop international law. The Italians also made the unusual proposal that Assembly decisions could be taken on the basis of a two-thirds majority vote rather than the unanimity which was eventually required by the Covenant.

The functions to be allotted to the League Secretariat were much less controversial, with earlier ideas that it might be given certain political powers quickly being forgotten. The Secretary-General (given the grander title 'Chancellor' in most early drafts) was essentially to be an administrator and co-ordinator of the activities of the League with those of other international organisations. The Secretariat was to have the role of gathering information, both in a general sense and, more importantly, whenever states referred disputes to it. One indication of the relative absence of conflict amongst the powers over the Secretariat came when a meeting of a special Organisation Committee — set up under House to draw up details of the administrative structure of the League — was able to conclude after only eight minutes' discussion.[57]

The League Covenant contains elements which embody all these principles, but it would be a mistake to see the League simply as an attempt to translate these ideas into their appropriate institutional forms. The Covenant that finally emerged in 1919 represents the outcome of a bargaining process involving many disparate elements and contending interests. It was, first and foremost, a compromise between the British and American viewpoints: one which managed to patch over the only partially concealed suspicions each nurtured about the other's true intentions. The extent of differences amongst the allies is illustrated by a report sent to Woodrow Wilson on 12 December 1918 by E. M. Hurley, his representative in the allied discussions on shipping and food distribution. Referring to the European leaders, he wrote:

What they are thinking about, as you are probably already aware, is the increased power of our shipping, commerce and finance. In every conversation the commercial question has come to the front . . . . The British are fearful that under a League of Nations the United States, with its present wealth and commercial power, may get the jump on the markets of the world.[58]

Nor did the British delegation speak with one voice: Hughes, the Australian Prime Minister, led a vociferous group which opposed any scheme to place the former German colonies under any form of international control.

Another complicating factor and, with the Bolsheviks, one of the two important but unseen presences at Paris, was the domestic American opposition to the League, led by Senator Lodge. Here too Anglo-American rivalries were apparent, but this time it was the Senate's opponents of the League who suspected Britain of plotting to dominate it. Despite this Lodge was secretly in contact with official British circles, who were left in no doubt of his belief that Wilson would not be able to obtain Senate ratification of the Covenant.[59] Apart from its apprehensions regarding British power, the Senate had several specific objections to the draft Covenant presented to them at the end of February after the League of Nations Commission had decided upon it. These were that domestic affairs were not explicitly excluded from the League's auspices, that the special relationship between the United States and Latin America, as embodied in the Monroe Doctrine, was not officially acknowledged in the Covenant, that the United States might be saddled with mandated territories against its wishes, and that the procedures by which states could withdraw from the League needed to be clarified. Later — after the Paris peacemakers had met most of these objections — opposition crystallised instead around Article 10 of the Covenant, which contained a diluted version of Wilson's long-cherished principle of guarantees of territorial integrity and political independence.

The Bolshevik Revolution had already made an important, if unwitting contribution to the League before 1919. By stealing most of Wilson's New Diplomacy clothes, including his demands for a peace without annexations and for open diplomacy, Lenin had compelled Wilson to concentrate all the harder on the one item the Bolsheviks had left him: the League of Nations. The Fourteen Points speech was itself made in response to the Bolshevik challenge, and there is more than a hint in British discussions of the League that it would have to be taken more seriously than many thought because it had come to represent a key element in the established powers' riposte to Bolshevism.[60] An even more specific rejoinder to the Russian Revolution was the creation of the International Labour Organisation, which won favour partly as a means of appeasing restive elements in the trade union movement who might otherwise be attracted to Communism.[61]

Three phases of bargaining over the Covenant took place in Paris. The first was in the weeks before the opening meeting of the League of Nations Commission on 3 February and involved primarily the British and American delegations. Next came the first series of meetings of the Commission, during which the basic draft of the Covenant was agreed. The final stage witnessed the reconvening of the Commission on 22 March to consider the series of amendments which Wilson wished to introduce following his return from the United States.

Wilson had insisted from the start that the establishment of the League should be the first item on the Paris agenda, an objective which Lloyd George, for his own reasons, decided to support, thus laying the foundation for Anglo-American collaboration in the actual drafting of the Covenant.[62] The ultimate fruit of this was the 'Hurst–Miller draft' of the Covenant: the version finalised by the British and American advisers on which the subsequent discussions were based. However, before the long drafting session between Britain's Cecil Hurst and the American David H. Miller on 1 February, a series of preliminary negotiations had taken place involving Wilson, House, Lloyd George and Cecil. The Australian, Canadian and Italian leaders also had some influence on the eventual draft.

Debate during this period revolved around two draft Covenants prepared by Wilson on 10 and 20 January. Cecil found that by adopting a somewhat liberal interpretation of his brief from the Imperial War Cabinet much of what Wilson had in mind could be accepted in a reworded form.[63] However, a number of crucial differences remained between British and American approaches which needed to be resolved. Wilson initially advocated a rather complicated system of compulsory arbitration for international disputes but found no difficulty in retreating from this position. Cecil's alternative suggestion was for a Permanent Court of International Justice, which he saw not only as an appeal court to which disputes between states could be referred but as a general court performing a wide range of useful functions in relation to all the lesser international organisations.[64] Similarly Wilson was able to accept with seeming equanimity a substantial amendment to his proposed system of guarantees of independence and territorial integrity. In the British alternative wording, which eventually appeared in the Covenant, the League members merely 'undertook' to respect and preserve territorial integrity and independence, rather than 'guaranteeing' them. One of the considerations which influenced the British in this was a desire not to see the territorial *status quo* frozen by international law.

Other issues proved more troublesome. Opposition to Wilson's proposals on mandates came not so much from Britain as from the Dominions, and several bitter confrontations were to take place before this question was resolved. A more fundamental Anglo-American conflict of interests was involved in Wilson's proposals for the League to be given powers to enforce the freedom of the seas and for discrimination in international trade to be outlawed. The British also found unacceptable Wilson's plan to give minor states significant representation in the League Council. The Hurst–Miller compromise managed to reduce all these points of contention to innocuous formulae, but this led Wilson, realising with dismay the extent to which his original ideas had been watered down, to make an unsuccessful eleventh-hour attempt to have the Hurst–Miller draft discarded in favour of one which more truly reflected his own approach.[65] As if to prove that the Hurst–Miller draft was a genuine compromise, shortly before this Lloyd George had also made an abortive attempt to abandon what he regarded as over-ambitious conceptions of the League and return to the earlier British idea of an institutionalised great power Concert.[66]

The League of the Hurst–Miller draft envisaged power as being concentrated in the hands of an Executive Council of the United States, Britain, France, Italy and Japan, who could invite any other member to attend should its interests be directly affected by the matter in hand. Collective security was provided for by a general undertaking to respect and preserve against aggression the territorial integrity and political independence of members, and by a specific agreement that states involved in a dispute would not resort to armed force until they had submitted their conflict to arbitration or inquiry by the Council. Breaking this latter agreement was to be regarded as an act of war against all other League members, who were to respond immediately by severing economic and financial relations with the offending state. The Council was to examine the logistics of military sanctions. All League members had the 'friendly right' of bringing to the attention of the Council any matter which threatened international peace. A permanent court was to be set up with competence to hear cases deemed to be 'suitable for submission to arbitration, and which cannot be satisfactorily settled by diplomacy'. The League was to have responsibilities in the field of disarmament, although these were left somewhat vaguely defined. The principle that partial disarmament was essential for the maintenance of peace was acknowledged, and the Council was required to formulate plans for the reduction of armaments and to look into the feasibility of abolishing compulsory military service. Where control of the arms trade was necessary 'in the common interest', this was to be supervised by the League.

Articles 17–20 of the Hurst–Miller draft broadened the League's range of responsibilities. Article 17 declared that the well-being of the peoples of the former enemy colonies was a 'sacred trust of civilisation' but made no stipulation that the colonies should become League Mandatories. The stress of this Article was rather on preventing the individual colonial power from enjoying exclusive rights to exploit the economic resources of the colonial territories and from being able to draw upon the colonial peoples to build up its army. Article 18 affirmed the need to establish fair working hours and conditions of labour, while Article 19 guaranteed the freedom of religion. Article 20 contained all that was left of Wilson's original dream of granting the League powers to supervise the freedom of the seas and promote free trade. It read in full: 'The High Contracting Parties will agree upon provisions intended to secure and maintain freedom of transit and just treatment for the commerce of all States members of the League.'[67]

Much of the Hurst–Miller draft found its way into the final Covenant, but a number of significant changes were made during the sessions of the League of Nations Commission from 3 February to 14 February and after Wilson's return from the United States on 14 March. A united front presented by the Brazilian, Serbian, Belgian, Chinese and Portuguese delegates forced Cecil to back down from his opposition to small power representation on the Council, with four places for such states being eventually agreed on. What was now an 'undertaking' to preserve the independence and territorial integrity of all League members was further diluted after renewed pressure from Cecil. In his view this Article still implied that the existing territorial *status quo* was frozen by law, which would make it more difficult to carry out such later territorial adjustments as might be needed in the interests of international order. More seriously, if the obligation had any concrete substance, he thought an automatic commitment to go to war to uphold it was entailed, which Britain was not prepared to accept.[68] Eventually Cecil agreed to an amendment of Wilson's which stated that in the event of aggression it would be left to the Council to 'advise the plan and the means by which this obligation should be fulfilled'.[69] This effectively rendered the Article innocuous because any action under it would have to be unanimously agreed by the Council, but this was still not enough to prevent the Article from later becoming one of the chief obstacles to the Covenant's ratification by the American Senate. Cecil's other concern, that the territorial settlement might become unduly sacrosanct, was met by a new Article (number 19 in the Covenant) which provided for the periodic revision of international obligations.

The disarmament article was subjected to detailed scrutiny, which led to one significant change.[70] Wilson had allowed his original call for the abolition of conscription to be toned down in the Hurst–Miller draft to meet Italian objections. Now the French declared their total opposition to any reference to this subject and so it was dropped. However, Wilson was able to secure the addition to the original article of an assertion that the private manufacture of armaments was 'open to grave objections'.

What were, in principle, the most important articles of the Covenant, those laying down the League's right to concern itself with any threat to peace, the provisions for peaceful settlement of disputes and the mandatory sanctions to be imposed against violators of these agreements, were all passed with few major alterations.[71] The French tried to raise again their proposal that some kind of International General Staff be created, but without success. The sole concession made to the French position was the establishment of a permanent Commission to advise on military matters. A greatly changed mandates article was also passed without much discussion, largely because its provisions had been worked out in advance during several acrimonious sessions before the League Commission officially commenced. The new Article set out clearly the principles that the League as a whole had an ultimate responsibility for the former enemy colonies, and that not just the 'well-being' (as in the Hurst–Miller draft) but the 'development' of these colonies was a 'sacred trust of civilisation'. The division of the mandated territories into three types according to their readiness for self-government was the central theme of the new mandates provisions.

The mandates article provided one instance where the Covenant ran counter to the central orthodoxy of international relations: the principle of each state's absolute sovereignty in its own domain – including its colonies. Another attempt to assert the existence of international standards of behaviour which, by implication, limited the freedom of governments to do as they pleased domestically was less successful. Wilson had proposed an article in which the League members agreed not to interfere with the free exercise of religion, nor to discriminate against people adhering to any particular religion or belief.[72] This was generally acceptable, but problems arose when

Japan's representative, Baron Makino, tried to graft on to it a statement opposing discrimination against aliens on account of their race. This was the only significant Japanese intervention in the Commission meetings, and Wilson had, in fact, been advised as early as November 1918 that the Japanese intended to raise the question of racial equality.[73] The Japanese proposal was anathema to the Australians and other members of the British empire delegation, who saw it as potentially threatening their policy of refusing coloured immigration. As Makino had hinted strongly that he regarded acceptance of his proposal as a necessary *quid pro quo* for Japanese support for the religious equality article, both in the end had to be dropped.

Two important sets of amendments were inserted in the Covenant after Woodrow Wilson's return to Paris on 14 March from his unsuccessful mission to win over the Senate. Wilson had been advised during his visit that four key changes to the draft Covenant might suffice to win him a Senate majority:

1. A specific affirmation that the Monroe Doctrine, one of the traditional pillars of American diplomacy, was not affected by the Covenant.
2. An explicit recognition of states' exclusive jurisdiction over their own domestic affairs.
3. Clear provisions by which states could withdraw from membership of the League.
4. An acknowledgement that states could refuse to become mandatory powers should they so wish.[74]

Wilson was clearly going to need substantial support in Paris if these amendments were to be passed without the entire Covenant being opened up for revision. The British were willing to help him out but at a price, which included his agreement to a somewhat weaker disarmament formulation, as had been demanded in a strongly worded Admiralty memorandum.[75] Following discussions between Cecil and the Americans on 18 March a new set of amendments was then presented to the reconvened League of Nations Commission, as a common Anglo-American position, although Wilson proposed his Monroe Doctrine amendment separately.[76]

The final stages of the drafting process remained, but these added little of substance to the Covenant as revised by the British and Americans. Perhaps the most significant change stemmed from another British initiative, which increased the emphasis on the League's role in matters other than security by making it the central co-ordinating and directing body over several other functional organisations. In other respects the last discussions did not augur well for the League. Further limitations were written into the collective security provisions, leading the French to declare that they would be obliged to depend on separate defensive alliances.[77] The Monroe Doctrine amendment was passed only with enormous difficulty and the Japanese failed again to have even the most innocuous reference to racial equality accepted. More generally, such optimism as had been present in earlier meetings had become soured by the 'sauve qui peut' atmosphere now prevalent in Paris and by the increasing likelihood that the United States would not ratify the Covenant.[78]

CONCLUSION

As a legal document the Covenant had many deficiencies. Some articles were ambiguous or contradicted other articles. The crucial provisions for collective security were full of loopholes. However, the criticisms of this nature that were made at the time (and are still occasionally repeated in the literature on the League) were misguided. States did not operate within the confines of a fully developed legal order, where, like tax evaders, they were merely engaged in an unending search for legitimate ways of attaining their ends. The fact that the Covenant could be interpreted as permitting some kinds of aggression in certain sorts of circumstances was immaterial, although anyone witnessing the battles in Paris over the precise wording of this or that clause might be forgiven for thinking otherwise. The significance of weak or ambiguous formulations in the Covenant was not that these might permit wars which a stricter wording would have prevented, but that they accurately reflected the doubts felt by most states about committing their security to the new system.

Indeed the League had, in a sense, failed in its primary purpose even before it had officially started, when London, Washington and Paris agreed to a tripartite system of alliances to guarantee French security, thus bypassing the League mechanism. When these alliances proved abortive following American failure to ratify the peace treaties, France continued to seek security outside the League framework. Hence in the all-important field of great power relations the League had effectively been ignored from the outset. It remained to be seen whether it might still have a role to play in less important aspects of peace and security as an alternative to traditional diplomacy.

Apart from its role as a provider of collective security, the League may be said to represent two points of departure in the history of international relations. Firstly, it embodied a limited consensus as to the existence of certain international standards of conduct which could be given some status in international law. More generally, it expressed an intention to extend the role of international law itself as, in the words of the Preamble to the Covenant, 'the actual rule of conduct amongst governments'. Secondly, it was an acknowledgement of the increasing range of common functional interests shared by states and the need for more effective centralised supervision of these. The subsequent history of international organisation was to be much concerned with both of these developments.

2 The League of Nations

At one level, the history of the League of Nations is synonymous with the often-told story of the failure of the Western democracies to oppose the aggression of the Fascist regimes and prevent world war. The international order established at Versailles was inherently unstable because the temporary weakness of Germany and Russia meant that the balance of power upon which it was founded was essentially artificial and impermanent and would come under increasing strain as those two states regained their strength. In so far as the League was associated with that order, it too would come under threat. Since the founders of the League always saw it as, above all else, a provider of collective security, there can be no real objection to an assessment of the League in these terms. However, at another level — the one with which we are most concerned here — the League was also an episode in the history of international organisation. Viewed in this light, what is most remarkable is that, far from the disastrous failure of the League leading to a hiatus in the growth of international institutions, it was followed by an unparalleled increase in their number and range of functions. So, while *an* organisation was discredited between 1919 and 1939, international organisation as a significant *process* in the relations amongst states may be said to have become firmly established during the same period. To understand how and why this was the case, four distinct aspects of the League need to be considered: its collective security operations, its role as cornerstone of the international legal order, its function as overseer and co-ordinator of a variety of economic, social and technical activities, and the development of its principal institutions.

THE LEAGUE AND INTERNATIONAL SECURITY

As many people have pointed out, certain basic flaws were always inherent in the abstract concept of collective security. It required states to be united in their determination to resist aggression, yet if such unity of purpose existed the reason for it would have vanished.[1] A dubious assumption is implicit in the concept — that it will always be perfectly clear that aggression has been committed and which state is the guilty party.[2] Only a collective security pact capable of bringing effective

24

sanctions to bear could hope for success, yet states are unlikely to establish such an obvious threat to their own monopoly of power.[3]

But those who controlled the League were practical statesmen not philosophers, and logical problems such as these are not the last word on the League's security functions, or its failure. The principal European leaders (if not Woodrow Wilson) had always seen the League as, at best, an institutionalisation of older methods of managing international relations, such as the balance of power and the Concert of Europe, rather than as the basis of a wholly new international order. Even these more cautious conceptions of the League failed to materialise when the absence of the United States, following the failure of the American Senate to ratify the peace treaty, prevented an effective balance of power from being built, and the assertiveness of smaller states both in the Assembly and in their demands for representation on the Council obstructed a return to an old-style great power Concert. This meant, as Lord Balfour noted in 1925, that conflicts amongst the major powers arising from 'deep-lying cause of hostility' were beyond the League's effective influence.[4] This problem was exacerbated by the fact that certain other great powers were not members throughout the League's life: Germany was not admitted until September 1926 and left in October 1933, the Soviet Union did not join until September 1934, Japan withdrew in 1933, Italy left in 1937 and several Latin American states were also absent for various periods. Yet a substantial security role remained, and it was the development of this in the 1920s which made the first ten years of the League appear at the time to be so promising.

The first difficulty encountered by the League was how to define its precise powers in peace and security matters. One complicating factor was the continued existence for several years after the war of the allied Ambassadors' Conference, which sometimes seemed to be a rival (and intrinsically more powerful) agency for ordering postwar international relations. This problem first arose when the League was asked to consider Yugoslavia's incursion into Albania in 1920, which some members doubted its competence to do when the issue was already on the agenda of the Ambassadors' Conference. On this occasion Albania declared that the League was the true successor to the European Concert (which had originally settled the Albanian question in 1915) and so it alone had the right to pronounce on Albanian affairs.[5] However, during the Greco–Italian crisis of 1923, Mussolini was able to claim that the League had no right to consider the matter because Greece had brought it before both the League and the Ambassadors' Conference, and the latter had precedence in Italy's opinion.[6]

Some of Europe's more tradition-minded diplomats were at first disinclined to grant the League any more responsibility than absolutely necessary. In 1921, for instance, Lord Curzon reproved the Persian Foreign Minister for writing to reassure the League's Secretary-General that a recent Anglo-Persian agreement was not incompatible with the Covenant. The only effect of such a letter, he maintained, would be to afford the League a pretext to sit in judgement on Persia's sovereign right to interpret its own treaty obligations in any way it chose.[7] Similarly, the allied powers in early 1920 refused to refer the Adriatic question to the League Council, arguing that to do so would imply that there was complete disagreement amongst the allies which diplomacy was unable to overcome and that a reference to the League under Article 11 (which mentioned situations threatening war) would 'start rumours of war unnecessarily'.[8] Taken at face value these observations seemed to negate the whole purpose of the League, which had been set up as a centre for diplomacy and as an alternative to war.

The withdrawal of the United States was followed by a widespread move to water down the crucial collective security provisions of Articles 10 and 16. The Canadian delegation presented a resolution on Article 10 to each of the first four Assemblies, initially in an attempt to have the Article deleted from the Covenant, later with the aim of having a restrictive interpretation placed on its stipulations. All these resolutions failed, but the Fourth Assembly version only received one negative vote and most governments came to accept it as an authoritative interpretation of their real commitments under the Article. A British Foreign Office memorandum in 1926 suggested that, whenever the League Council had to determine the Article 10 obligations of League members, it should have due regard for the 'geographical situations and special conditions' of each state, and that members themselves were free to decide whether they would contribute to any military action under Article 10, with Council recommendations merely being 'taken into consideration'.[9] The provisions for automatic sanctions in Article 16 were similarly weakened by a number of Assembly resolutions interpreted by the Foreign Office to mean that sanctions were not obligatory, although states should 'co-operate loyally' in any collective action under Article 16.[10] Conversely, efforts to strengthen the League's collective security provisions were generally doomed to failure. Cecil was unable to secure the adoption of a Treaty of Mutual Assistance, which would have made collective security operate on a regional rather than a global basis, and have ensured that sanctions under this system would be more effective.[11] In 1924 the 'Geneva Protocol', which would have provided for compulsory arbitration of disputes, also failed, primarily because of British objections.[12] The success of the high-sounding but toothless Kellogg–Briand Pact in 1928 and the more important Locarno Treaty in 1925 did, however, help to create an illusion that the League was being strengthened rather than weakened. The Locarno Treaty involved Britain, France and Germany in a series of mutual guarantees of the Franco—German and Belgo—German frontiers (but not Germany's eastern frontiers), while the Kellogg—Briand Pact was a declaration by the foreign ministers of the USA and France, eventually signed by all but a few states, which renounced war as an instrument of policy. The Locarno Treaty marked a high point of co-operation amongst the European powers but the other document was soon forgotten after the failure of an attempt by Britain and France in 1929 to have the Pact incorporated into the League Covenant.

As the League came to be a more familiar fixture on the international landscape, so the powers began to make greater use of it for a vast range of purposes, although there were still some who, like Lloyd George, privately bewailed the results of this trend: 'It [the League] should have been much more informal, like the Supreme Council. As it was, it had weak links spreading everywhere and no grip anywhere.'[13] In general, however, after this initial wariness had diminished, the powers developed the habit of passing on for League consideration a range of disputes and other international problems which for various reasons they were unable or did not wish to resolve by normal diplomatic means. For instance, in 1920 London brought the dispute between Sweden and Finland over the Åland Islands before the Council because it saw this as the safest way of dealing with an issue of some delicacy (given Soviet interest in the Islands), without causing dissension amongst the Western powers.[14] Here one concern was to use the League to give an aura of legitimacy to the territorial distribution which had resulted from the break-up of the Tsarist empire. The same aim was apparent in an attempt by the allies to place the short-lived breakaway state of Armenia under League protection, although on this occasion the League Council declined the allied request, arguing that the League did not have the resources to undertake tasks of this magnitude.[15]

Even Lloyd George discovered a use for the League in 1921, when he threatened Yugoslavia with League sanctions during a conflict between Yugoslavia and Albania.[16] Lord Balfour was later to claim that the peaceful settlement of this dispute had only been possible because both states could accept the disinterestedness of the League's bodies, including the Commission of Inquiry which was set up to investigate the matter.[17] This was a fairly typical example of the self-congratulatory tone which accompanied some of the League's successes in the 1920s and which helped to create a popular faith in the League's efficacy that was in fact founded on illusion. In this case it had been a great power ultimatum to a smaller state which had forced a settlement and one, moreover, in a situation where both sides had been genuinely anxious to reach a border demarcation.

Other issues were passed to the League by the Supreme Council or the Ambassadors' Conference: sometimes because the powers didn't want to spend time on them; sometimes because the questions involved were intractable and handing them over to the League was a convenient and legitimate way of evading responsibility for them; occasionally because they were an unwanted source of friction amongst the powers themselves; and sometimes because they genuinely called for a lengthy process of impartial investigation. Numerous border disputes in eastern and central Europe, Anglo-French differences over Upper Silesia, the Saar Territory and French nationality policies in Tunis, and the problems of stabilising the international economy, all ended up with the League Council for one or more of these reasons. Its normal work-load also included countless smaller problems arising out of its peace treaty responsibilities for various minority populations.

The resolution of questions of this kind led Britain's Foreign Secretary, Austen Chamberlain, to declare in 1925 that his respect for the League had increased now that he had seen it at work, not 'on one of those great problems which excite most attention but on those little problems which if we do not settle them might be a great trouble in the world'.[18] This raises the difficult question of how to assess the value of much of the League's work in the 1920s. The League existed in part to prevent minor crises from escalating into major confrontations between the powers, but one can only speculate as to whether any of the crises of the 1920s contained the seeds of a larger conflict which the League could therefore be said to have averted. However, the more ambitious claims made for the League during this period were probably unjustified. Sarajevo had led to war in 1914 because many circumstances had combined to produce an atmosphere of war-preparedness in Europe. In the 1920s almost the opposite conditions prevailed.

A number of conflicts during the 1920s were referred to the League by one of the disputants, of which the most serious were between Greece and Italy in 1923, Greece and Bulgaria in 1925, and Bolivia and Paraguay in 1928. Other incidents involving hostilities included a recurring clash between Poland and Lithuania and a dispute between Britain and Turkey concerning sovereignty over the province of Mosul on the Turkey–Iraq border.

The Greco-Italian incident began in August 1923 when three Italian diplomats were assassinated in Greece, prompting Mussolini's government to send a bellicose ultimatum to Greece with a set of demands which included the payment of a 50 million lire indemnity within five days.[19] When the Greek government did not submit immediately, Italian troops occupied the Greek island of Corfu, whereupon Greece appealed to the League Council. To most objective eyes the injured party in this case was Greece, with Italy clearly having violated the Covenant by its immediate recourse to arms. The case was thus an important test for the League, since Italy still had pretensions to great power status. However, France was at this time involved in a somewhat similar action to Italy's, having occupied the Ruhr in an attempt to enforce payment of Germany's reparations bill, and was in any case in no mood to condemn a fellow great power in order to bolster some abstract principle of collective security. The Council therefore contented itself with passing the matter to a Commission of Inquiry of the Ambassadors' Conference, simultaneously prejudging the result by ordering Greece to deposit 50 million lire in a Swiss bank pending the Commission's findings.[20]

The contrast with the Council's handling of the Greco–Bulgarian affair two years later was instructive. This began in September 1925 when Greek troops crossed into Bulgaria after a shooting incident on the border. Strong diplomatic pressure from Britain and France, acting through the League Council, brought about a rapid ceasefire and a Commission of Inquiry was appointed to investigate the causes of the conflict and the amount of reparations which should be paid. In contrast to the Greco–Italian dispute, when the Council in effect determined in advance both Greece's responsibility and that Italy should receive the full indemnity demanded, the Council in 1925 declared that 'all necessary care and deliberation should be employed in ascertaining the facts and fixing the amount of reparations due'.[21] Moreover, whereas in the Corfu incident a legal commission went some way towards condoning Italy's premature resort to force, in the Greco–Bulgarian conflict Briand, then President of the Council, stated as a general principle that 'in the case of a territory violated without sufficient reason reparations are due, even if at the time of the event the party committing the violation believes that the circumstances justified his act'.[22] However, although the outcome of this affair was hardly the triumph for collective security it was claimed as at the time, it did illustrate the advantages of the existence of the League in a crisis involving two small states where the great powers had no vital interests and so could act in concert. The Bulgarian government was confident enough to be able to instruct its troops not to resist the Greek incursion once it knew that the League Council was taking up the matter. Even Greece, which could justifiably feel aggrieved at the double standards which seemed to apply to similar behaviour by great and small powers, was partially appeased when it received economic aid, arranged through League auspices.[23] Both Greece and Bulgaria benefited from the appointment of a small group of observers to arbitrate over any frontier dispute for two years after the ceasefire – a forerunner of contemporary UN peacekeeping operations.

The Bolivia–Paraguay conflict, which developed into a major war in the 1930s, revealed that the League's sphere of action was mainly limited to Europe and that it could do little in Latin America without the support of Washington. When the first fighting occurred in 1928, the matter was placed before the Council by the League Secretary-General, Sir Eric Drummond, in a rare use of his personal initiative.[24] However, the Council merely reminded the two sides of their Covenant obligations and passed the issue on to a pan-American institution, which unsuccessfully attempted to resolve the dispute by arbitration.[25] When the conflict reached the level of full-scale war in 1933 — a war in which 100,000 were to die — the League was more extensively, although equally ineffectively, involved. It sent out a Commission of Inquiry, attempted vainly to bring about a conciliation, appointed a special Advisory Committee on the matter and tried to enforce a cease-fire by organising (with some success) an arms embargo first against both sides, then against Paraguay alone after it had rejected Assembly proposals on the war.[26] Although the United States participated in the arms embargo, it refused to join either of the investigative bodies and it was clear to the disputants that these lacked credibility without an American presence.[27]

By the end of the 1920s the League had developed a number of techniques which it had used with varying degrees of success in several conflicts. There were established routines for investigating disputes, conciliating the parties and keeping the peace in the aftermath of the fighting. These had, on occasion, even been backed by the threat of sanctions. Yet, as the major crises of the 1930s unfolded, the League seemed increasingly irrelevant, to a point where such a momentous event as the loss of statehood by one of its own members, Austria in 1938, could take place virtually without comment from the League. But in most cases it was not so much that the League did nothing — the 1930s witnessed the entire range of possible League responses to crises — but that what was done was always too little or too late.

The limitations of the League were perhaps demonstrated most clearly in the first great crisis of the 1930s, when Japanese troops overran Manchuria in 1931.[28] Japan had a legitimate military presence in Manchuria to protect its interests in the South Manchurian Railway, and it was an explosion on the railway, allegedly detonated by Chinese soldiers, which sparked off the Japanese move into Manchuria. Although it was revealed years later that the whole incident had been engineered by the Japanese army as a pretext for the invasion, blame at the time appeared to be more evenly divided. The League Council at first hoped to be able to deal with the issue in much the same way as it had handled the Greco—Bulgarian conflict — as an 'accidental' outbreak of fighting which both sides wanted to be peacefully resolved. China appealed to the League under Article 11 of the Covenant, where the emphasis was on conciliation, rather than immediately resorting to the collective security and enforcement provisions of Articles 10, 15 and 16. The Council's first move was to call for a ceasefire and withdrawal of Japanese troops. When the Japanese did not withdraw and further Council meetings (attended for the first time by an invited American delegation) were fruitless, it was decided on 10 December to send a League Commission under Lord Lytton to investigate the dispute. Meanwhile Japan's advance continued, and in January 1932 new fighting broke out in Shanghai. This led China to make a fresh approach to the League, this time invoking Articles 10 and 15 and appealing to the Assembly rather than the Council. The Shanghai affair proved to be merely a temporary episode, but Japan, increasingly dominated by militarist elements, established a separate puppet state in Manchuria, 'Manchukuo', on 9 March. Nearly seven months later the report of the Lytton Commission was published. Although it refused to countenance international recognition of Manchukuo, it called for Manchuria to have autonomous status within China, with a significant Japanese influence over its administration. The report strove to maintain a similar evenhandedness throughout, but its adoption by the Assembly on 24 February 1933 was followed on 27 March by Japan's withdrawal from the League.[29]

The Manchurian crisis brought into sharper focus than any previous conflict the range and complexity of the problems faced by collective security in general and the League in particular. The first area of confusion concerned whether Japan could be identified as a clear-cut aggressor. Throughout the crisis Japan was acknowledged to possess legitimate interests in Manchuria and, especially at the beginning, many were inclined to believe that the Chinese had brought the conflict upon themselves[30] — a belief bolstered by frequent Japanese assurances as to their limited intentions, which the Council had little option but to accept.[31] Secondly, and inevitably in a crisis sparked off by a great power, a variety of larger political considerations outweighed the immediate issue for the other powers. Britain and France were anxious not to take any action that would be opposed by Washington, while in the United States the State Department was influenced by the possibility that League opposition to Japan might have an adverse effect on the domestic balance of power in Japan between civil and military factions.[32] None of the powers was really willing to confront Japan, while, in accordance with a long tradition, one section of the British Foreign Office seemed more concerned initially lest French duplicity might enable Paris to gain some advantage over London in its relationship with Japan.[33] A third problem, and one for which the institutionalised character of collective security was partly responsible, was the considerable delay in implementing the various stages of the League's consideration of the matter. Japan was able to use a range of delaying tactics including legal quibbles throughout the crisis,[34] while the length of time taken for the Lytton Commission to be constituted and arrive in China occasioned bitter complaints from the Chinese.[35] Finally, the crisis clearly revealed the Eurocentric nature of the League. Several influential British diplomats argued, in effect, that the fundamental principles on which the League was based were not applicable to this conflict because the Japanese had not yet 'assimilated the ideas of international relations which have guided British policy since the war',[36] and because, given Japan's special rights in Manchuria, 'the ordinary canons of international intercourse have no application in Manchuria'.[37]

The crisis which effectively broke the League as a force of any significance in the important political questions of the time was the Italian invasion of Ethiopia on 3 October 1935. Although Ethiopia was a sovereign member of the League, Mussolini's government had long seen it as occupying a special, quasi-colonial position in relation to Italy. As early as 1926 Ethiopia had had occasion to protest to the League because of an Anglo-Italian agreement over the exploitation of Ethiopia's economic resources. In 1928 Italy and Ethiopia signed a treaty which included provisions for arbitrating any fresh dispute that might arise between them, but the crisis of 1935 occurred essentially because Mussolini no longer had any interest in a peaceful settlement of disputes with Ethiopia and was determined upon a course of annexation. It began with clashes between Italian and Ethiopian soldiers in the Wal-Wal region of Ethiopia in December 1934. After an initial show of reluctance, Italy was eventually persuaded to seek a peaceful solution under the terms of the 1928 treaty. However, Italian pressure on Ethiopia continued unabated, with a build-up of troops in neighbouring Italian Somaliland and a series of delaying tactics designed to prevent the commencement of the arbitration procedures. On 16 March Ethiopia appealed to the League under Article 15 of the Covenant, which dealt specifically with disputes which had not proved amenable to arbitration or judicial settlement.[38]

For France and, to a lesser extent, Britain, the Ethiopian crisis from start to finish posed a number of genuine dilemmas which strongly influenced their actions after this point. If Italy under its imperious leader were pushed too far this could lead to a great power conflict, with the inevitable risk of a general conflagration, in the name of an organisation whose purpose was to prevent war. Moreover the real danger in Europe, as was becoming ever more apparent in 1935–6, was Hitler's Germany, and Italy was a significant factor in the European balance of power whatever side it might eventually support. On the other hand, should the prestige of the League be seriously damaged by great power inaction over Ethiopia this might have equally unfortunate consequences, including a widespread increase in insecurity. As France's Prime Minister, Pierre Laval, put it in July 1935: 'France's entire European policy is based upon the League of Nations. The League of Nations is the basis of the Locarno Treaty, which is an essential element of French security, and it is within a League framework that the agreements which bind us to our friends in Central Europe are inserted.'[39]

So when Ethiopia appealed to the League in March, the initial Anglo-French response was to renew efforts to have the affair settled by arbitration rather than by the League Council. Mussolini was now prepared to feign a willingness to accept arbitration, especially as he believed that he had received a number of signals from Britain and France suggesting that they might acquiesce in an eventual Italian conquest of Ethiopia.[40] Hence the League Council did not effectively take up the Ethiopian crisis until September, although Britain and France had in the meantime been involved in informal negotiations with Italy.[41] They had also begun to consider the prospects and likely consequences of applying military sanctions against Italy should Article 16 of the Covenant eventually be invoked. Laval and Sir Samuel Hoare, Britain's Foreign Secretary, privately agreed that sanctions should be limited to economic and financial measures to be applied 'cautiously and in stages'.[42] But in public Hoare made a strong speech at the Assembly in the hope that this might deter Italy from the action it was so obviously contemplating. During September a number of League Committees were established to investigate and try to resolve the dispute, while the Commission of Inquiry into the Wal-Wal incident reported its findings on 3 September, which effectively exonerated both parties. Another League Committee (investigating one of Italy's pretexts for the legitimacy of its pressure on Ethiopia) recommended on 18 September that a League Commission should be appointed to promote internal reform in Ethiopia. But the futility of all such gestures of conciliation was demonstrated when Italy launched its invasion on 3 October. Four days later the Council decided that Italy had gone to war in violation of its Covenant obligations, and on 11 October the Assembly appointed a Committee to co-ordinate the imposition of sanctions.

From this point, the international response to the invasion proceeded at three different levels, which were not always in harmony with each other. At one level, the various League institutions and special Committees concentrated primarily on the sanctions question. At another, Britain and France, while also involved in organising sanctions, continued their behind-the-scenes efforts to obtain an agreed settlement, efforts whose course was critically influenced by important differences between the two powers.[43] At the third level, public opinion, which had been so strongly emphasised by Woodrow Wilson when the League was established, played an important, though by no means always a helpful role, nor one in which the different national publics, especially in Britain and France, spoke with the same voice.

The principal economic sanctions imposed were an embargo on exports of war materials to Italy, a prohibition of all Italian exports and a ban on the granting of any loans to Italy. Although inevitably these measures were not universally observed, they did inflict a significant degree of damage upon the Italian economy. However, it soon became clear that for Italy to be forced to withdraw from Ethiopia more severe measures would have to be considered. Debate at Geneva came to focus on the prospects of imposing two additional sanctions: prohibiting oil exports to Italy and closing the Suez Canal to Italian shipping. The second was never a real possibility: Britain and France, who controlled the Canal, both regarded this as clearly a military rather than an economic sanction and one that would very probably lead to war.[44] But an embargo on oil was another matter and was very nearly enforced. -

The League Co-ordinating Committee on sanctions advocated an embargo on oil on 9 November. Romania, which supplied 40·6 per cent of Italy's oil, and the Soviet Union, which supplied 16 per cent, both agreed to support an embargo so long as it was universally observed.[45] Supplies from another important source, Iran, were effectively controlled by Britain, so prospects for a successful embargo looked good. But although the American Secretary of State, Cordell Hull, had publicly supported the idea of an embargo, Sir Samuel Hoare had very serious doubts as to whether American oil producers would not take advantage of the United States' non-membership of the League to make up any deficiency in Italy's oil imports caused by an embargo.[46] More important, however, was the constant fear in both London and Paris that an oil embargo might provoke Mussolini into a 'mad dog act' — that is a declaration of war.[47] Britain was also concerned that, should this happen, she would not be able to count on the support of France, which was going through a period of political turmoil and where public opinion, partly influenced by newspaper campaigns, appeared hostile both to Britain and to any idea of war with Italy.[48] It was largely these considerations, combined with worries about Britain's lack of military preparedness, that led to the abortive 'Hoare–Laval Pact' in December, by which the two powers would have attempted to settle the crisis on terms favourable to Italy.[49] A contemporary interpretation by a British diplomat present at the meeting between Hoare and Laval suggests that calculations about the longer-term security of Europe were a major factor:

To force France against her will to fight would have meant a definite break of the Anglo-French understanding and therewith risked the end, not only of the League of Nations but, far more serious, of European civilisation. Europe would have been left at the mercy of Germany when the time came for Berlin to move.[50]

However, opinion in Britain, which was strongly pro-Ethiopian, forced Hoare to resign when details of the Pact were revealed, and eventually at the end of February 1936, after a League committee of experts had concluded that a universally supported oil embargo would prove effective against Italy within three and a half months, Britain decided to support oil sanctions. This caused consternation in France, coming as it did at the same time as the developing crisis over Germany's re-militarisation of the Rhineland. But French apprehensions proved to be premature as resistance in Ethiopia quickly collapsed before oil sanctions could be introduced. On 10 May the Ethiopian emperor, Haile Selassie, cabled the League that he had decided to end the war, prompting, amongst many other responses, Guatemala's immediate withdrawal from the League because 'events have demonstrated the impossibility of putting into practice the high ideals aimed at when the League was founded'.[51]

The Ethiopian crisis deserves the relatively detailed coverage it has received here because of its impact on the League and because it represents the only fully genuine collective security action undertaken by either the League or the UN. It also demonstrates some of the inherent problems of the central theme of collective security — that states undertake a general and open-ended commitment to unite against any aggressor — in a situation where action against one state could jeopardise the balance of power against another, far more dangerous aggressor. In the event the chief error of the powers, particularly Britain, lay in their inability to reach a clear-cut decision either for or against firm opposition to Italy. The best illustration of this does not involve sanctions but the other side of the coin: assistance to Ethiopia. In 1930 the League had passed a draft Convention agreeing to give financial support to states suffering aggression but this had never come into force.[52] Ethiopia appealed for financial assistance on 1 November 1935, arguing that 'relying upon the guarantee of collective security embodied in the Covenant, the Ethiopian Government had created neither arsenals nor arms and munitions factories'.[53] Britain's ambassador to Ethiopia strongly urged the government to support the Ethiopian request, but Sir Samuel Hoare replied that as the League as a whole (which was waiting for a lead from Britain) refused to agree to a collective loan to Ethiopia, Britain would not do so unilaterally.[54] Ethiopian military resistance to Italy was, in fact, surprisingly effective for some months,[55] and after the ceasefire Ethiopia's delegate to the

League argued strongly that lack of financial support to purchase weapons and munitions had been the decisive factor in the Ethiopian defeat.[56]

A final illustration of the problems faced by the League in its efforts to promote international security is to be found in its pursuit of disarmament: seen by many in 1919 as an essential component of an effective collective security system. An early success in arms control was achieved at the Washington Conference of November 1921, when each of the major powers agreed to limit its naval strength by keeping it within a predetermined ratio *vis à vis* the other powers. However, this agreement was reached outside League auspices and when the League attempted to fulfill its commitment under Article 8 of the Covenant to promote general disarmament measures, it immediately encountered some fundamental problems. Some of these were of an essentially technical nature, such as how to compare different types of armaments for arms limitation purposes, how to distinguish between 'offensive' and 'defensive' weapons and how to supervise commitments to disarm to ensure that they were fully executed. But the fundamental political problem was that agreements to limit arms at the levels current at any given time would please only those who were basically satisfied with the status quo at that time, while they would be unacceptable to those, such as Germany, who wished to revise the existing order and whose current military strength was well below its true potential. All of these issues came to a head at the League's Disarmament Conference which met from February 1932 until the end of 1934 (although its effective end was in October 1933 when Hitler took Germany out of the Conference and the League). The Conference, which was attended by an American delegation, was always overshadowed by the Manchurian crisis and even more by the tightening Nazi stranglehold on Germany but even before Hitler became German Chancellor in January 1933 the Conference had failed to produce any results other than to confirm a 1925 agreement that poison gases should be prohibited in warfare. The Conference had merely served to confirm the fact that substantial disarmament, like collective security in general, required an atmosphere of mutual trust — an exceedingly distant prospect in Europe of the 1930s.

After the Ethiopian crisis the League lingered on with increasing irrelevance until 1946. Its last act in the collective security field, one that blended petulance and farce, came at the end of 1939 when, with all due solemnity, it expelled the Soviet Union for its attack on Finland. Hitler's aggressions, the Spanish Civil War and even Turkey's annexation of part of Syria in 1936 had all taken place with only marginal League involvement. Many explanations and excuses have been offered for the League's failure: it lacked universality, with the

United States never a member and Germany, the Soviet Union, Japan, Italy and several Latin American states absent for various periods; it had to cope with crises of extraordinary magnitude and frequency at a time when the popular mood in the democracies was against war and the worldwide depression made even the cost of economic sanctions seem intolerable; the association of the League with the Versailles Treaty made it automatically unpopular in Germany; the Covenant was a flawed document from the start, with too many ambiguities and loopholes for would-be aggressors; or alternatively it was too ambitious and always impracticable in a world of sovereign states. From another perspective, to talk of the League's failure is meaningless when what really happened in the 1930s was that Anglo-French diplomacy failed in the face of relentless aggression, with the League merely one of the instruments available to the two powers. If so, it was never an instrument in which they seemed to invest much confidence: the combined annual budget of the League, the ILO and the Permanent Court was seldom greater than 6 million dollars — barely the cost of a single cruiser. The 'realistic' argument that the same lack of solidarity amongst states which seemed to make a League of Nations necessary also doomed it to failure may well be correct. It may have been unrealistic to hope for substantial disarmament or any significant diminution of their sovereignty from the powers. But it was perhaps not unduly idealistic to expect that they would at least enable the League to perform its limited functions without the constant need to justify every expense to the world's treasury officials.

THE LEAGUE AND INTERNATIONAL LAW

In a strict sense the League's role in relation to international law should not be distinguished from any of its other functions. The Covenant was part of international law and the central theme of all aspects of the League's work was that states should be guided by rules of conduct. So whenever the League attempted to carry out its peace treaty obligations to minorities by organising plebiscites or investigating disputes; whenever it tried to decide rules and guidelines to govern international economic relations or such matters as the postwar refugee problem; when it drew up international conventions on environmental and ecological questions, such as the regulation of whaling or controlling the pollution of the seas by oil; when it devised more comprehensive international regimes in areas like communications and transit, preventing the spread of epidemics, or controlling the drug traffic: in all such work it was undertaking tasks which, at the very least, had important implications for international law. But apart from such activities, which in strict legal terms provided 'evidence' of the existence of a rule of international law, rather than actually creating law in themselves,[57] certain aspects of the League's work had a direct and longer-term influence upon the role of law in international relations.

A major innovation was the creation of the Permanent Court of International Justice. This had received relatively little consideration prior to the Peace Conference, being one of several ideas which only gained momentum during the negotiations in Paris.[58] The Court, which commenced operations in 1922, consisted of eleven (later fifteen) judges selected by both the Council and Assembly to 'represent the main forms of civilisation and the principal legal systems of the world'.[59] The Court had the capacity to make judgements on disputes brought before it and to give 'advisory opinions' when requested by the League. These opinions were not formally binding upon states but in practice acquired almost as great a legal significance as the actual judgements. The Court heard sixty-six cases between 1922 and 1939, of which twenty-eight were requests for advisory opinions. Fifty of the cases were filed before 1932. States had the option of declaring in advance their acceptance of the Court's jurisdiction of certain classes of dispute, an option taken up with various reservations by forty governments, with jurisdiction otherwise being voluntary.

Many of the cases stemmed from friction arising out of the peace treaties, especially where Polish—German relations were involved. Some created significant precedents, as when a 1928 advisory opinion on the courts of Danzig appeared to imply that individuals had rights under international law, thus rejecting the traditional doctrine which only accorded such rights to states.[60] However, the Court was not (nor was it really intended to be) a major force for peace and stability. As with any legal system, the effectiveness of international law is in direct proportion to the existence of order and a sense of community in the society which it serves.[61] Rather, the importance of the Court was threefold. It showed that a standing international court did have a part to play in promoting orderly international relations in conditions where there was already a strong underlying desire for order. It was a significant landmark in the gradual acceptance by states that rules had a place in international politics. It also developed a body of jurisprudence which played a part in the adaptation of international law to changing circumstances — which, in a sense, acted as a new source of international law itself.

Although the League was far from being an international legislature, other aspects of its work did have some significance for the creation of international law. 120 international conventions were concluded by the League before 1939, not to speak of eighty agreed by the ILO.[62] This did not mean that they automatically became binding upon states since they all required (and often failed to obtain) ratification by the sovereign body of each state; but they were none the less important in bringing about subtle changes in the process of law formation in international relations. Traditionally law had 'emerged' from the practice of states. Now, without the old system being displaced, a new element had been introduced (as had been the intention of the Hague Conferences) in which both the general principles and the fine details of international law were debated by states, with attempts being made to arrive at a consensus view. Such a view could not fail to be regarded as important evidence of the existing state of international law, even if it was not, strictly speaking, law itself.

An attempt was made to give the League a more clear-cut role in defining and co-ordinating the current rules of international law, but this was opposed as 'a very dangerous project' by no less a League supporter than Lord Robert Cecil.[63] However, following an initiative from smaller states, a committee of experts was later set up to begin the codification of international law in such areas as nationality, territorial waters and the rights of aliens.[64] A conference on codification was held at The Hague in 1930, but this was generally admitted to be disappointing and the next Assembly abandoned the attempt at codification.[65]

The League's most intimate involvement with international law came in the various experiments in international administration of the interwar years. Apart from its responsibilities in economic and other functional areas, which are considered shortly, the League administered the Saar Territory, supervised the government of Danzig, and oversaw the mandates system.

The Saar Territory was an economically important area on the Franco—German border which was claimed by both countries. The League governed it for fifteen years, at the end of which it organised a plebiscite, as required by the Versailles Treaty, to determine the wishes of the inhabitants. The League's governing Commission of five members had full powers during its administration, with the League Council only empowered to intervene in emergencies. However, the inhabitants had the right (of which they made the fullest possible use) to petition the Council directly. Because of the impending plebiscite everything the Commission did acquired from the start a heavy political content amongst the mostly German-speaking population.[66] The plebiscite, as expected, gave the Territory back to Germany, with a massive Nazi campaign making the result even more inevitable.[67] The League administration, though always unpopular with the Saarlanders, had in fact been both fair and efficient, but ironically the only real beneficiaries of this were the Nazis, who thus gained an orderly and profitable addition to their domain.

The port of Danzig was established as a free city in order to meet

Polish demands for access to the sea without actually ceding the city, with its mainly German population, to Poland. It was not directly governed by the League but placed under its protection, with a High Commissioner to act as mediator in disputes. This ensured that Danzig had a complicated and unwieldy governmental structure, with the elected Danzig government, Polish officials with various rights and powers including control over foreign policy, the semi-independent Habour and Waterways Board and the League High Commissioner all occupying separate positions of power. The League Council was itself available as an appeal court of the last resort, although in practice Danzig's problems were the most constant items on its agenda, especially before June 1925, when the procedure was changed to allow the High Commissioner to deal directly with the experts and technical agencies of the League.[68] Matters came to a head with the Nazification of Danzig that commenced in 1933. The position of the High Commissioner, as the sole buffer between the Nazis and their victims, became increasingly difficult. For a time the League Council attempted to support the High Commissioner, Sean Lester, in his efforts to uphold the League's authority and the Danzig constitution. But, as he complained in 1936, 'each meeting of the Council during the past year was followed by an intensification of the policy which has been deplored by the Council'.[69] By 1937, after Lester's departure for the Secretariat, the Council had effectively abandoned Danzig to its fate.

Article 22 of the Covenant had distinguished between three categories of mandate for the former enemy colonies, taking into account 'the stage of development of the people, the geographical situation of the territory, its economic conditions and other similar circumstances'. The detailed implications of this were later worked out in a series of charters adopted by the Council, which in each case gave the mandatory power 'full powers of legislation and administration', with the common requirement that it provide an annual report on its administration to a League Commission of eleven experts on colonial affairs. The different types of mandate were listed as C mandates (South-west Africa and Germany's Pacific territories) which were virtually indistinguishable from colonies, B mandates (other African colonies of Germany) where several restrictions on the mandatory power were laid down, and A mandates (Palestine and Trans-Jordan, Syria and Lebanon, Iraq) which had a wide range of different provisions. The charter for Palestine, for example, included the requirement to put into practice the Balfour Declaration, which had promised a Jewish national home there. The Iraq mandate stipulated that Iraq should be given its independence as soon as possible.[70]

Several problems were evident in the mandates system from the start. It did not bring about a new order for colonies as a whole since it applied only to former enemy colonies. This made the mandated territories appear, with some justice, to be merely spoils of war. The fact that the League Commission was given only marginal and indirect powers of supervision added to the impression that what was really going on was a form of covert annexation by the victorious powers. There was virtually no consultation in advance with the peoples living in the territories, in sharp contrast with the care that was taken to ascertain the views of the new nations and minorities in Europe. But despite these flaws advice from the Mandates Commission was generally taken seriously by the mandatory powers, partly because of the extreme tact employed by the Commission in its dealings with the powers.[71] Seen from the 1980s, when colonialism is all but finished, the mandates system may seem paternalistic and hypocritical. Yet it did serve to focus public attention upon the colonies and help to create the climate of opinion which later made decolonisation inevitable.

THE ECONOMIC AND SOCIAL FUNCTIONS OF THE LEAGUE

From one perspective the League was simply the international reflection of the expansion of governmental powers and functions domestically. As governments came increasingly to concern themselves with wider issues than raising revenue and defending the realm, so they employed ever greater numbers of officials in ever more complex bureaucracies to deal with these matters. And so it was inevitable that they responded to the international dimensions of these problems in the same manner: by establishing international bureaucracies. This, rather than collective security, was the true growth area in international organisation, with more than 60 per cent of the League's budget going to its economic and humanitarian work by 1939.[72]

It is part of the tragedy of the League that its complete failure in security matters was matched only by its inability to affect the rise of economic nationalism and the ensuing global economic crisis of the 1930s. Here, however, it had the partial excuse that it was not originally intended to play a substantial economic role. Apart from Article 16, which imposed automatic economic sanctions against aggressors and required states to give each other mutual support to minimise any loss caused by sanctions, the sole reference in the Covenant to economic matters is a few words in Article 23 calling for equitable treatment of the commerce of all League members. The other economic functions grew out of the needs of the time, the most urgent of which in 1920 was reconstruction. The League did enjoy some success in this field, particularly in the case of the financial reconstruction and stabilisation of Austria, a problem handed over to the League after the powers had failed to reach agreement on it elsewhere.[73] The

Financial Committee of the League was involved in similar exercises in Hungary, Bulgaria and Greece.

However, the more deep-seated problems of the world economy eluded all attempts at international solution whether within or outside the League framework. Between 1920 and 1933 several major conferences on global economic affairs were held under League auspices, while a variety of so-called 'technical' committees consisting of experts in economic and financial matters were in almost constant session. An American delegation attended many of these meetings. One of the biggest conferences, in 1927, adopted resolutions which recognised global economic interdependence and set out certain fundamental principles (for example the removal of import and export restrictions) that were thought to be central to improving growth and reducing unemployment.[74] But governments paid little attention to these eminently sensible proposals, as even the League's own self-congratulatory ten-year progress report was obliged to recognise.[75] The last of the great economic conferences, held in London in 1933 in circumstances of desperate worldwide crisis, failed after five weeks when the United States, the only state with the necessary economic power to make a stabilisation scheme work, refused to become involved.[76] After this the League's agencies tended to concentrate on narrower research activities.

Economic reality in the 1930s dictated that unless Washington were prepared to assume the kind of responsibility for underwriting the global economic order that it did after 1945, there could be little hope of any real progress. The predominant liberal-capitalist ideology insisted on the need for international competition – despite the prevalence of national economic protection – while the emergence of alternative ideologies provided an additional source of disharmony over economic matters. For instance, at one point a special League committee was set up to examine 'economic aggression', which was seen as arising from the supposedly unfair advantage of countries with state-controlled enterprises.[77] However, to set against its failure to influence national economic-policy formulation, the League probably did constitute a necessary stage in the transition between an international free-for-all and the system which lasted for thirty years after 1945. It compiled an enormous amount of essential information, enabled an exchange of ideas and experiences and revealed some of the technical and structural difficulties that would have to be overcome if a new economic order was to work.

The League was rather more successful in its other 'technical' activities. It established major institutions such as the Health Organisation and the Communications and Transit Organisation, as well as numerous committees on such matters as the drug trade, refugees, the traffic in women and children and intellectual co-operation. The important non-members of the League, including Germany, participated in most of these activities from the start. Although the new technical organisations did not supplant all of the existing international unions, as had originally been intended, they did make a significant contribution to the development of international regimes in their respective fields. For instance, the 1921 Barcelona Conference on Communications and Transit adopted a Convention on freedom of transit across international boundaries which achieved a high level of subsequent ratification, although another Convention on international waterways failed to be ratified.[78] Other conferences reached agreement on a wide range of lesser communications issues, although in some instances they met with complete failure, as in 1931. In health matters the League continued and expanded the work done by earlier sanitary authorities to such effect that it provided the model for the UN's World Health Organisation. It established new procedures for combating epidemics, sent out several large medical units to China, standardised a great number of medicines, stimulated interest in nutrition problems and initiated studies of child welfare, public health training and many other subjects.[79] The League was similarly active in a wide range of other technical areas, although, as ever, the League agencies were constrained by lack of adequate financial support. The comparative success of the League in its functional work led the Bruce Committee, which investigated possible reforms in this area in 1939, to propose that all this part of the League's work should be brought under the supervision of a single agency, to be called the Central Committee for Economic and Social Questions — a proposal taken up when the UN was established.

Special mention should be made of the International Labour Organisation as the only significant part of the League structure to survive intact after 1945. Originally envisaged as a safety valve against the spread of Bolshevism, its constitution gave it potentially far-reaching functions, a fact of which its energetic first Secretary-General, Albert Thomas, took fullest advantage. Its Constitution began with the firm, if debatable, assertion that 'the League of Nations has for its object the establishment of universal peace, and such peace can be established only if it is based upon social justice'. Hence, apart from its basic role in attempting to improve working conditions, the ILO was given some responsibility for pursuing such reforms as the prevention of unemployment and the provision of an adequate living wage. Its influence, such as it was, upon states was enhanced by the fact that most of the non-members of the League, including the United States, did join the ILO. Perhaps more significantly, the trade union movement was a powerful ILO constituency with a strong interest in promoting the ILO's cause. The ILO had no powers to compel states to meet the minimum international standards of labour legislation set by its conferences, a fact which went some way to explaining the general willingness of states to take at least some notice of its conclusions.

THE STRUCTURAL FRAMEWORK OF THE LEAGUE

One aspect of the League which had, for better or worse, a lasting impact on future international organisations and on the wider conduct of diplomacy was the structure of its principal bodies, the Council, Assembly and Secretariat. In each case the basic pattern set in the League was maintained in the UN as well as in several regional organisations.

The Council's prospects of becoming an institutionalised great power Concert had vanished when the Peace Conference accepted the principle of four Council seats for smaller states on a non-permanent basis. There had been a brief period dating from the 1925 Locarno agreements when it had seemed that an informal Concert system might be emerging out of regular meetings between the British, French and German Foreign Ministers. But to some extent these sidestepped the formal Council sessions rather than utilising them, although the three Foreign Ministers did begin the practice of attending the Council in person during this period.

Once the principle of small power membership of the Council had been first conceded, it inevitably made the acquisition of such a place a matter of prestige and even, for some states, a major foreign policy goal. The Assembly had decided in 1920 that the main criterion in the allocation of non-permanent places should be equitable geographical distribution.[80] But this did not dispel the competitive attitudes of the smaller states concerning Council places, and only accentuated an already evident tendency towards the formation of regional blocs in the Assembly and the other League bodies. This issue came to a head with the crisis in 1926 over Germany's admission to the League (and an automatic Council seat) which led to claims for permanent Council membership from Brazil, Poland and Spain. An attempt was made to appease them by increasing to nine the number of non-permanent seats (which had already been increased in 1922 to six), to include a new category of three 'semi-permanent' seats, whose holders could be re-elected by a two-thirds majority of the Assembly. This did not satisfy Brazil and Spain, who both resigned from the League, although Spain returned within two years.

Another aspect of the Council which worked against any prospect of it functioning as a high-powered international directorate was its obligation to deal with a mass of detailed work arising out of the peace settlement. The finer points of the problems of Danzig, the Saar and a host of minorities all became monotonously familiar to the Council during the 1920s, one reason, perhaps, why the Soviet Union was to insist that the Council's UN successor should confine itself to security matters. Later the Council acquired an unforeseen role as one of the actual arenas of conflicts amongst the powers rather than an agency for effecting compromises amongst them. This tendency was inevitably strengthened by the public sessions of the Council, which were originally hailed as a victory for Woodrow Wilson's 'open diplomacy' philosophy.

In contrast to the determination shown by the smaller states at the Peace Conference to have a significant influence upon the composition and powers of the Council, the Assembly had received very little attention, largely because it had always been seen as the lesser of the two bodies.[81] In most eyes the Assembly was to be essentially a forum for discussion through which Wilson's 'world public opinion' would make itself felt, especially as it was envisaged that the three Assembly delegates permitted for each state would not be government officials. None the less, despite the generally low expectations of the Assembly, it was allocated a number of functions in the Covenant which gave it the potential for developing a significant role in the future. Article 3 gave it the capacity to deal with 'any matter within the sphere of the League or affecting the peace of the world'. Article 11, which in later years tended to be invoked in preference to the more stringent collective security provisions of Articles 10, 15 and 16, gave members the 'friendly right' to bring before the Assembly, as well as the Council, any circumstance threatening international peace. There was also a provision, added as an afterthought to Article 15, for disputes to be transferred from the Council to the Assembly, if so required.

However, these formal provisions were far less important in establishing the Assembly's significance than a series of precedents set in the first Assembly, which opened on 15 November 1920. The most crucial of these was the Assembly's decision to meet every year, as against the assumption at Paris that meetings would be held only every four years. The delegates at the first Assembly were generally leading statesmen, rather than the assorted representatives of various walks of life who were originally supposed to constitute it. This inevitably gave it a much higher political awareness and a collective determination not to accept a subordinate role. The first fruits of this came when the Assembly appropriated for itself the overall financial control of the League, a responsibility that had not been specifically allocated by the Covenant.[82] This immediately gave the Assembly something of the aura of a parliament as well as a means of intervening in almost every aspect of the League's work. In some instances the first Assembly gave itself this right more directly, as when it requested the Council to present future Assemblies with a report on its work in the previous year and when it referred to its committees such matters as the League mandates, which were supposedly the sole responsibility of the Council. Finally the first Assembly immediately captured the public imagination: it had a glamorous air about it and seemed to be the repository of the remaining early idealism which had surrounded the League concept.

During its lifetime the Assembly tended to be the principal initiator of much of the day-to-day business of the League. Its committees not only promoted various projects in the League's technical agencies and drew up many international conventions but also formulated potentially important proposals in the security field, such as the abortive Geneva Protocol. It also requested the Council to pursue various matters, and in general saw itself as the overseer of all aspects of the League's work. On important political questions the requirement for Assembly votes to be unanimous sometimes prevented action, though nothing like as often as had once been feared.[83]

Only three disputes were directly referred to the Assembly, with results which in general did not suggest that such a large organisation could play a useful role where tact and diplomacy might be needed more than verbal belligerence. This was particularly the case of the first dispute, the fighting in Shanghai during the Manchurian crisis, where a highly nationalistic and sensitive government such as Japan's could hardly be expected to take kindly to criticism from smaller states. The Assembly debates were one of the factors leading to Japan's withdrawal from the League, as they were also in prompting Paraguay to withdraw after the Bolivia–Paraguay dispute had been referred to the Assembly. The third instance, the Soviet invasion of Finland, came when the League was already virtually irrelevant, although its action in expelling the Soviet Union was likewise an expression of moral indignation rather than a well-thought-out attempt to resolve the crisis.

Despite its role as initiator and supervisor of general League policy, the Assembly's real significance still lay in its performance of the function for which it was principally designed: an international forum for the expression of 'world public opinion'. The Assembly did not feel itself to be restricted in any way as to the subjects it could legitimately discuss, and for the first time most major issues could be debated by the community of states as a whole. Views inevitably differ about the value of this exercise. One contemporary observer writes that as time went on the Assembly 'tended to lose its parliamentary character altogether. The "declaration", carefully prepared, neatly typed and often monotonously read took the place of speeches. The proceedings became not only decorous but dull.'[84] But to another writer, the Assembly was 'very much what the representative body of an international organisation should be' and the influence of the small powers generally 'temperate and constructive'.[85]

The third part of the League's structure was its Secretariat. The Covenant had nothing to say about the recruitment of the Secretariat or how it was to perform its various functions. Many assumed that officials would be recruited from the existing body of national diplomats and that these would retain a primary allegiance to their state rather than to the League. The first Secretary-General, Sir Eric Drummond, attempted from the start to establish a rather different principle, borrowed from his experience in the British Civil Service, which made League officials responsible to the League rather than their own countries and called upon governments to accept that their nationals had to pursue the League's interest during their period of office. In return officials themselves were supposed always to act impartially. Another principle laid down at an early stage was that members of the Secretariat should be drawn from as wide a geographical area as possible.

Inevitably practice did not always match the theory. Places on the Secretariat assumed a political significance from the outset, as the major blocs in the League strove to ensure that their interests were well represented. For instance, when the Frenchman Joseph Avenol replaced Drummond as Secretary-General in 1933, Italy, Germany and the smaller states as a whole each demanded and received the 'compensation' of an additional place on the Secretariat.[86] Moreover, as Drummond's biographer notes: 'In a sense, Secretariat positions and places on temporary or permanent League bodies . . . were a type of spoils system manipulated both to pay off political obligations as well as to assure the continual loyalty or assistance of a particular power.'[87] A worse problem was that some members of the Secretariat blatantly pursued the interests of their own countries. This was especially the case of the fascist states, but even Drummond himself maintained close links with the British Foreign Office, frequently informing London about his Secretariat business and sometimes about his dealings with other powers.[88] He was also given access to confidential documents by the Foreign Office — a useful privilege in view of the League's lack of a diplomatic service of its own but one that inevitably gave him a somewhat Anglocentric view of affairs.[89] In general, however, Drummond worked to prevent any suspicion that he was simply allowing the League to be used as an instrument of British policy. A more common problem with the Secretariat, especially under Avenol, was that it tended to see the first interest of the League as survival intact without the withdrawal of any of its members, especially the important ones, which meant that it normally supported the advocates of appeasement.

In two respects the Secretariat demonstrated the value of having a permanent body of international officials. It frequently served as a useful and necessary channel of communication between the many parts of the League, including the national delegations. And over the years it became a repository of information and experience concerning the unique problems of international organisations. Indeed it may say something for the validity of the concept of the impartial international Civil Servant, not to speak of the continuity between the League and the UN, that many League officials later took up employment with the UN.

CONCLUSION

That the failure of the League did not doom the whole process of international organisation is, as has been remarked, at first sight suprising. There are three main reasons why the powers should not have thought it futile to try again with the United Nations. The first is that it was easy to point to various defects in the Covenant and to believe that these could be remedied in the subsequent organisation. If in addition the United States became a member, the overall imbalance of power that had made the war possible could be decisively corrected. Secondly, it was clearly going to be increasingly difficult for the major powers simply to ignore the voices of the smaller states in matters where the latter felt they had a significant interest. The League had provided one means of catering for this new element of 'international democracy', and it was difficult to envisage how else but in an international organisation meeting continuously all states could accept that their views had an equal chance of being heard.

Finally, the League had been established as a response to several clearly perceived problems and these showed no sign of going away. Indeed the tasks which seemed to require co-operative international solutions had grown in number, as even the briefest comparison of the Covenant with the UN Charter indicates. It was possible to see the League not as having failed but simply as having made a start, if not an especially promising one. This was clearly the case in such areas as the development of international law and the range of issues arising out of economic interdependence, but even in relation to international security matters the League had developed a variety of peacekeeping mechanisms which could, perhaps, be built upon.

3 The United Nations in World Politics

There was never any question in the minds of the allied leaders about whether a new collective security system would be created after the Second World War. Equally there was no prospect of this new organisation being built on the existing League structure: this was generally discredited and wholly unacceptable to the Russians, who had been expelled from it. But although references to the League at the principal allied meetings which drew up the Charter were few and usually disparaging, it is clear that the League experience was too relevant to be ignored, especially by the professional diplomats responsible for working out the details of the new organisation. Hence the United Nations, in its essentials, was seen as an improved League, rather than a departure from it.[1]

The greatest improvement, at least as envisaged by the major allies, was that the UN would be unequivocally based on the principle of a great power Concert. The most ambitious variant of this would have had a World Council of the powers overseeing a series of regional councils on which the powers would be represented alongside states within each region. This was originally Churchill's approach and was also favoured by Roosevelt.[2] The reasoning behind it was that collective security would work most effectively within a regional framework, which would ensure that members of each regional organisation had an interest in co-operating to settle disputes. But both the British Foreign Office and the American State Department were hostile to the regionalist concept and succeeded in persuading their leaders to abandon it. However, the Concert principle remained at the heart of all allied proposals for a United Nations Organisation, with the three major powers agreed on a minimum necessity that they themselves should be empowered to veto any UN enforcement action, which effectively limited the sphere of action of the UN to smaller states not allied to a major power. The American administration feared that the crude power politics underlying this position might prove unacceptable to the American people, not to speak of the Senate, which had rejected the League, and its public utterances concentrated on projecting a more idealistic, Wilsonian image of the UN. The United States' actual policy came to combine, somewhat uneasily, these two conceptions. One historian's view of the effect of this is that: 'The genuine tension between these two approaches remained concealed for most of the Second World War. After the war, the conflict became explicit, and a major source of the cold war.'[3]

A second theme to emerge from the deliberations in Washington and London was that the UN should have a greatly enlarged role in economic and social matters. This stemmed from an awareness that a major international effort was going to be needed to meet the immediate problems of postwar economic reconstruction; from a widespread feeling that some international safeguards should be instituted to counter blatant and extreme violations of human rights of the kind committed by the Nazis; and from a general belief that poverty and economic inequality helped to create stresses 'leading to dangerous crises and even war itself'.[4] The League was generally thought to have been successful in these areas and the Bruce Committee's report on establishing a new economic and social organisation was taken up by the allied committees engaged in planning the postwar world.[5] Indeed, some functional organisations, notably the Food and Agricultural Organisation (FAO), were established before the UN itself. The Soviets did not share the Anglo-American enthusiasm for the UN to have what they regarded as 'an endless number of superfluous functions', but they did not push their opposition on this question too vigorously.[6]

Whereas the Covenant had been essentially an Anglo-American creation, the Charter was much more an exclusively American document. British policy toward the UN was dominated by the desire to prevent a re-enactment of the United States' rejection of the League, which meant that London was not prepared to resist any American proposals on the UN. The Soviets were in a position somewhat analogous to that of France in 1919. Their overriding concern was to safeguard their future security against Germany, a concern that in their view could only be met by achieving a favourable postwar balance of power. They saw the UN as basically irrelevant to this need.[7] Moreover, although Moscow too had an interest in ensuring American involvement in postwar international relations – it was the Soviets who insisted that the UN be sited in the United States rather than in Switzerland – they were aware of the danger that the UN, with its many Latin American and British Commonwealth members, could become a tool of Anglo-American diplomacy. Hence the twin objectives of their UN policy were, if possible, to enable it to perform a useful role in relation to Soviet security requirements but primarily to prevent it from being turned into an anti-Soviet instrument. In furtherance of the first aim, the Soviets pressed for the UN to have genuine military teeth in the form of an international air force and overseas base facilities,[8] while their second and more important priority led to demands for multiple

Soviet seats in the UN and especially for the absolute right of veto for great powers.

Much has been written on the underlying motives of Washington's UN policy. At one extreme is the view that Roosevelt saw the UN as an important element in an overall strategy of working towards a postwar world which would provide 'the orderly international setting that America's open-market economy demanded for continued success'.[9] At the other extreme is the idealistic, Wilsonian view of Roosevelt's Secretary of State, Cordell Hull, that the UN would be the means of doing away with the spheres of influence, alliances and power politics of the old diplomacy.[10] Somewhere in between is the notion that Roosevelt saw the UN as 'a means of bringing the Soviet Union into the family of nations and of continuing to promote Soviet cooperation at low as well as high levels of government'.[11] In other words, the UN was to be a means of extending the life of the wartime alliance beyond the end of the war and widening its sphere of operation. The true picture probably combines elements of all these as well as other interpretations. Many Americans had a say in the UN policy and their ideas sometimes conflicted. In particular Truman seems to have adopted a more uncompromising approach than Roosevelt towards Moscow, and to have had a conception of the UN that was less in tune with the power political realities of the time.[12] Above all, the imperative need to be able to 'sell' the new organisation to the American people trapped the administration into advocating quite different public and private versions of the UN, a source of much general confusion and some bitterness in Moscow.

The context in which the Charter was drafted differs from its predecessor in two important respects. The creation of the UN was kept separate from the peacemaking process, and the UN was not given specific responsibilities for upholding the postwar settlement. The drafting of the Charter was also a much more professional and considered affair. American planning for a new organisation began with the start of the war in Europe, more than two years before Pearl Harbor.[13] By 1943 thinking had crystallised around the conception of a universal and general-purpose organisation rather than the earlier regionalist idea, and the allies declared their intention to establish such an organisation at the Moscow Conference in October. The details of an agreed allied Charter were worked out by professional diplomats at a conference at Dumbarton Oaks during August and September 1944. The sensitive question of the precise extent of the veto was left to the top-level Yalta meeting in February 1945, where a formula was agreed by which all decisions except procedural matters required 'the concurring votes of the permanent members', although parties to a dispute were required to abstain where the Charter's peaceful settlement provisions were being invoked — but not where there was any question of sanctions.[14] At Yalta the Soviets also reduced their Dumbarton Oaks demand for all sixteen constituent republics of the Soviet Union to be represented to a claim for three seats, which was accepted.

Another question not decided at Dumbarton Oaks was the nature of the trusteeship scheme which was to replace the League of Nations mandates system. The American Joint Chiefs of Staff had insisted that this matter should not be raised until Washington had decided the future of some of the Japanese islands in the Pacific, which in their view were so vital to American security that they should be annexed without any element of UN supervision.[15]

The Dumbarton Oaks Proposals were presented to the San Francisco Conference of fifty nations held between April and June 1945. American Secretary of State Stettinius, who opened the Conference, made it clear that the Proposals represented the 'highest common denominator amongst the four sponsoring nations' and were not negotiable except in the case of marginal details.[16] In particular no enforcement action could be taken against the wishes of a major power: 'those peace loving nations which have the military and the industrial strength required to prevent or suppress aggression must agree and act together against aggression. If they do not agree and act together, aggression cannot be prevented or suppressed without major war.'[17] The Soviet delegation actually went beyond the Yalta formula and maintained that the powers had an absolute right of veto, even over whether the Security Council should be able to discuss a particular question. But, as at Versailles, the smaller states resisted several aspects of the great power conception of the UN. Australia's Deputy Prime Minister, who was the first of the smaller powers to speak, made five central points which were constantly reiterated in subsequent speeches and in private negotiations. These were a refusal to accept the absolute right of veto; an insistence that the powers of the Assembly should be much greater, that it 'should become the central organ or the forum in which the conscience of the peoples of the world should have its most potent expression'; a claim for some states below the level of great powers who had made important contributions to the war effort to have the right to what today would be termed 'middle power' status in the new organisation with various special rights and privileges; a demand that the proposed Economic and Social Council (ECOSOC) should be made one of the principal organs of the UN; and an assertion that the trusteeship principle should be extended to all colonies, not just the former enemy colonies.[18]

After much argument and a personal appeal to Stalin, the Yalta voting formula was accepted. But the smaller powers achieved more or less what they had demanded for the Assembly and ECOSOC. Although the trusteeship system was restricted primarily to former enemy colonies, a concession was made by which the colonial powers could voluntarily place territories under the system. There was, in addition, a general declaration (Article 73 in the Charter) by which the colonial powers accepted a wide range of responsibilities in their colonies, including the promotion of political and economic development, and also promised to transmit regular reports to the UN Secretary-General.

COVENANT AND CHARTER

To some extent the Charter is much less relevant in understanding the subsequent functioning of the UN than was the Covenant in relation to the League. This is partly because the UN developed in ways not foreseen in the Charter and mostly because the great power unanimity that was required for the UN's security system to function was seldom available. But the Charter did represent an evolution in thinking about the role of international organisations which deserves consideration.[19]

This is perhaps most apparent in the frequent references in the Charter to human rights. These were not mentioned in the Covenant: a reflection of the traditional international legal doctrine which made individual rights solely the concern of governments. The Charter upheld this principle in Article 2, whose seventh paragraph prohibited UN intervention in matters 'essentially within the domestic jurisdiction of any state'. This inevitably created an inherent conflict with the human rights clauses, which seemed to imply a UN right of intervention in the domestic affairs of states, and Article 2.7 has been invoked on many occasions, both in questions relating to human rights, such as racial discrimination in South Africa, and in colonial issues.[20] Much turns upon the meaning of 'intervention', with those states most jealous of their sovereignty maintaining that the UN has no right even to discuss their internal affairs (including colonial matters when this was a live issue). However, although the UN's actual powers in the human rights field are strictly limited, increasingly it has become a major forum for the expression of opinion on this subject.

A second difference between the League and the UN concerns the much greater importance attached by the UN to economic and social questions. The General Assembly, rather than the Security Council, is given primary responsibility here, although in practice the spectacular development of the UN's economic and social activities has taken place in a more or less autonomous fashion. The history of the UN's social and economic activities is considered shortly, but one preliminary point may be made here. ECOSOC, UNESCO and the other agencies, like the human rights machinery, were important not so much for any specific achievements, although there were many, but for their impact on the expectations of states, the kind of claims made upon international organisations, and the gradual change in the nature of the major issues in international politics from security questions to economic and social matters.

A third difference, which has already been mentioned, was the changed colonial regime. This reflected a fundamental shift in thinking away from the condescending references in the Covenant to 'advanced nations' and 'peoples not yet able to stand by themselves' to a clear affirmation of the responsibility of colonial powers to prepare their subject territories for independence. Again this heralded and indeed helped to usher in a new era and new agenda in international relations.

What was intended to be the most important change – the transformation of the Council into something closer to a great power Concert or even directorate[21] – never materialised because, as was rightly believed in 1945, this would only work given harmonious relations amongst the powers. This inevitably enhanced the position of the Assembly, which could now take decisions on the basis of a two-thirds majority. In other respects the Covenant and Charter greatly resemble each other – they have identical structures, both are based firmly on the principle of voluntary association amongst sovereign equals, many of the commitments of members are virtually identical, and the UN Secretariat is a continuation of its League equivalent, albeit with marginally greater powers. The real changes occurred in the international political and economic context within which the UN was to function: changes whose magnitude was only dimly perceived in 1945.

TO THE KOREAN WAR

From the beginning the UN was decisively affected by the developing cold war atmosphere between its two most powerful members. This influence was all-pervasive but perhaps most crucial in the growing tendency in Washington to regard the UN as an important part of its overall strategy *vis-à-vis* Moscow. Even before the first General Assembly opened in London on 10 January 1946, a State Department memorandum had hinted at the possibility of using the UN in this way.[22] The bluntest and perhaps most cynical statement of the policy of employing the UN as part of a first, diplomatic phase of resisting Soviet expansion came in a State Department memorandum on 1 April 1946:

The Charter of the United Nations affords the best and most unassailable means through which the US can implement its opposition to Soviet physical expansion. It not only offers the basis upon which the greatest degrees of popular support can be obtained in the US but it will also ensure the support and even assistance of other members of the United Nations. If, as may occur, the United Nations breaks down under the test of opposition to Soviet aggression it will have served the purpose of clarifying the issues before American and world opinion and thus make easier whatever future step may be required by the US and other like minded nations in the face of a new threat of world aggression.[23]

The Soviets were themselves adopting an intransigent stance even over relatively mundane issues such as the choice of the first President of the Assembly and the first Secretary-General, so the stage was set for the UN to become a major arena of the cold war confrontation between the two powers.[24]

The first question before the Security Council on 19 January 1946 brought an immediate great power clash. Iran had complained that Soviet troops, still present there under the wartime arrangements, were sponsoring a separatist movement in northern Iran. The Soviets denied this and, suspecting Anglo-American collusion with Iran, promptly brought counter-charges against Britain claiming that Britain was interfering in the internal affairs of Greece, where its troops were based at the request of Athens. The Iranian matter was resolved peaceably, at least for the time being, but the crude and blatant nature of the Soviet response led to a bitter Security Council debate on Greece.[25] On 18 March the Iranian question came up again after the Soviet troops had not been evacuated by the stipulated deadline of 2 March, with Washington bringing strong pressure on Iran to raise this in the Security Council.[26] The meeting saw the first Soviet walk-out, and also the first attempt by the UN Secretary-General, Trygve Lie, to claim more than merely administrative powers, when he presented the Council with a memorandum containing legal advice which the Council chose to ignore.[27] The Iranian crisis subsided after the withdrawal of Soviet troops in May, but Greece continued to concern the UN. In December 1946 Athens complained to the Council that Albania, Bulgaria and Yugoslavia were aiding the Communist guerrillas in Greece, prompting the Council to appoint its first Commission of Inquiry to look into the complaint. In September 1947, after repeated Soviet obstructionist tactics, the United States managed to transfer consideration of the Greek situation to the General Assembly, setting an important precedent thereby. The Assembly established an eleven-nation Special Committee on the Balkans (UNSCOB), nominally to assist the four governments to co-operate in settling their disputes, but in fact to bring pressure on Greece's northern neighbours.[28] Here again, whatever the rights and wrongs of this affair, it was clearly another instance of the UN being employed as an arm of American diplomacy, especially in relation to the Truman doctrine of taking on Britain's role of aiding Greece, which was enunciated on 12 March 1947.

Apart from the cold war, the UN was also influenced from the start by the other great theme of the postwar era: the movement against colonialism and racial discrimination. The first such issue concerned the conflict in Indonesia between the Dutch colonial authorities and the *de facto* Indonesian Republican government. The Netherlands, in the first of many such claims by colonial powers, asserted that the UN was precluded from discussing the matter by Article 2.7, as Indonesia was within Dutch domestic jurisdiction.[29] The Council managed to avoid pronouncing on its competence to take up the question and appointed a three-nation Good Offices Committee in an attempt at conciliation. Although the Committee succeeded in arranging a truce, this was soon violated by the Dutch and the Security Council upgraded the Committee into a Commission for Indonesia with greater powers. After strong pressure from Washington in the UN and elsewhere, the Netherlands agreed in March 1949 to proceed rapidly towards full independence for Indonesia.[30] This was clearly a case in which the existence and character of the UN influenced the behaviour of the two principal actors, the Netherlands and the United States, and also the eventual outcome. The Netherlands was plainly affected by the rising tide of criticism, especially from Asian countries, who were prepared to go as far as organising sanctions. The United States, while not wishing to antagonise the Netherlands, was unwilling to allow Moscow the propaganda victory of posing as the greatest friend of liberation movements. Moreover the mere fact of US membership of the Security Council meant that Washington had to become involved whether it wanted to or not,[31] although a 1950 State Department policy statement on the UN hints that the Department was not too averse to the opportunities Security Council membership gave it for extending American influence:

UN membership makes it not only legitimate but indeed a duty for the US, as a leading UN member, to concern itself with world problems wherever they may occur. This provides a solid basis for bringing US influence to bear in such distant places as Iran, Indonesia, Palestine, Korea, Greece, the Italian colonies, and the underdeveloped areas of the world.[32]

The UN also played a part in bringing to independence and delimiting the boundaries of the former Italian colonies in Africa, after the major powers had passed this matter to the General Assembly in 1949 following their own failure to reach agreement upon it. In all other questions involving the remaining colonies, the General Assembly acted as an important forum for the expression of opinion to a point by the

1960s when it had virtually made anti-colonialism the prevailing orthodoxy of the international community.[33] Linked with its campaigns on this issue was a growing effort to single out racism as a crime against humanity. As early as 1946 South African discrimination against its citizens of Indian origin was brought to the attention of the General Assembly, while later its policies of apartheid made it a prime target of the anti-racialist movement. As with colonial questions, governments accused of racial discrimination were able to claim that this was purely a matter of their domestic jurisdiction under Article 2.7, but many states, particularly those with liberal democratic governments and a free press, showed some sensitivity to international criticism. The exact role of the UN, as against other factors, in influencing governments to change policies is hard to determine. It is doubtful whether the credit for any single case of decolonisation or amendment of practices deemed racialist can be attributed solely to the UN. However, to a much greater extent than the League Assembly, the General Assembly did finally — for better or worse — approximate to Woodrow Wilson's ideal of a forum for the expression of what can only be termed 'world public opinion', a phenomenon which few could ignore.

The ending of Europe's empires, especially Britain's, provided other work for the UN from its earliest days. In 1947 Britain decided that it could no longer bear the sole responsibility for the intractable problems of Palestine, for which it still held a League Mandate and, fearing Soviet obstruction in the Security Council, on 2 April 1947 asked for the subject to be considered by the General Assembly. This sparked off a long and involved sequence of events over the next two years, whose repercussions are still being felt today.[34] The General Assembly's first action, in a resolution of 15 May 1947, was to establish the UN Special Committee on Palestine (UNSCOP) to carry out a lengthy and exhaustive investigation. UNSCOP reported its findings to the General Assembly in September, including two opposing sets of proposals for the future of Palestine.[35] The plan suggested by the majority of UNSCOP was for the partition of Palestine into an Arab state, a Jewish state and an independent City of Jersualem, with an economic union between them. The minority proposals were for a federal state to be established with Jerusalem as its capital. After further deliberations the partition plan was presented to the General Assembly at the end of November and, largely because of massive American pressure, was approved, and a UN Commission for Palestine was set up to implement it. However, the Arab states had made it clear throughout 1947 that they would not accept a Jewish state in Palestine under any circumstances, and none of the supporters of partition was prepared to underwrite the settlement by providing the enormous financial and military support that would evidently be required to bring about an orderly transference of power. In particular the United States, where opinion at the highest levels was divided over the wisdom of partition,[36] found itself on the horns of a dilemma. President Truman had made it clear that the United States should not undertake economic or military commitments to Palestine except within a UN framework,[37] but a UN force in Palestine could well involve Soviet troops being legitimately introduced 'into the heart of the Middle East'.[38] In addition there were the conflicting demands of its major ally, Britain, and a strongly pro-Jewish public opinion to contend with. One line of opinion in the foreign affairs establishment, notably that of the Policy Planning Staff under George Kennan, one of the most influential US policymakers during the period 1946—9, urged that the partition plan should be ditched because of the damage it was doing to US relations with Britain and the Arab world, and also because it was thought that the United States was being drawn into a potentially enormous commitment to Israel.[39] However, this was opposed by others, particularly those with major UN interests such as Dean Rusk, and their line appears to have been given the greatest weight in State Department advice to the President, which in any case supported Truman's own predisposition towards a Jewish state.[40]

When the partition plan encountered obstacles in the Security Council, the United States shifted its position towards supporting a temporary UN trusteeship over Palestine. But on 14 May 1948 the Jewish community in Palestine declared the existence of the state of Israel and Truman, without consulting the State Department, decided to grant it immediate recognition.

This was far from the end of the UN's involvement in the affairs of Palestine. Several UN officials were to be killed in the coming months, including Count Bernadotte of Sweden, who had been given the post of UN Mediator with the task of ending the Arab-Israeli war which had broken out upon Israel's self-proclamation. Much later the first large UN peacekeeping force was to be established in the Middle East, and the affairs of the region continued to dominate UN proceedings in the coming decades. But the crucial UN role (and possibly the UN's most significant impact at any time on world affairs) had been during 1947—8. The state of Israel and all the conflicts which have attended it from birth might well not have existed without strong American backing. Yet few, if any, clearly definable American economic or strategic interests were served by this emphatic support for a Jewish state — rather the opposite. A general sympathy, in which Truman shared, for the plight of the European Jews played an important part.[41] But in Kennan's view American policy towards Palestine had also become intertwined with American attitudes towards the UN: 'we are deeply involved . . . in a situation which has no direct relation to our national security, and where the motives of our involvement lie solely in past commitments of dubious wisdom and in our attachment to the UN itself'.[42]

Kennan's interpretation is to some extent borne out by a memorandum to the President in March 1948 by Truman's influential special adviser, Clark Clifford. After asserting that 'the United Nations is a God-given vehicle through which the United States can build up a community of powers in Western Europe and elsewhere to resist Soviet aggression and maintain our historic interests', he pointed to the high expectations of the UN held by the American people. These considerations meant, in his view, that the United States should firmly uphold UN decisions, in particular the partition resolution: 'In order to save the United Nations for our own selfish interests, the United States must promptly and vigorously support the United Nations actions regarding Palestine.'[43]

The culmination of the American policy of utilising the UN as an important instrument in its overall diplomacy came with the Korean War, which was also a turning point for the UN itself. Ironically, Washington's first use of the UN in relation to Korea was intended to reduce American commitment there, when it submitted the Korean problem to the General Assembly in September 1947.[44] In 1948 the Assembly called for the unification of Korea under a democratically elected government, establishing a Commission to work towards that end. Following North Korean aggression against South Korea on 25 June 1950, a hurriedly summoned Security Council meeting was able, in the absence of the USSR,[45] to take the first steps towards a US-led United Nations intervention in Korea. Amongst the factors responsible for Washington's prompt and decisive action was (especially on the part of President Truman) a determination to avoid any semblance of a repetition of the League's lack of resolution over the Manchurian and Abyssinian affairs, with the consequent damage to the UN's prestige, although others, such as General Bradley, Chairman of the Joint Chiefs of Staff, recognised from the outset that an intervention in Korea would be essentially an American operation 'under the guise of aid to the United Nations'.[46] Within weeks the earlier General Assembly resolutions in favour of unification were being cited as providing a pretext to press home the counter-attack and force the downfall of the North Korean regime itself.[47] The decision to do this had the effect of transforming the American/UN war aims from the limited collective security objective of repelling aggression to the larger American interest of unifying Korea under a pro-Western government, which eventually led to China's entry into the war.

So far as the UN was concerned, the Korean war had several consequences. At the time it appeared to many that the UN had successfully fulfilled its collective security obligations: it had passed the test which the League had failed in the 1930s. Ultimately, however, assessing claims of this kind depends upon a judgement (beyond the scope of this book) of the deterrent effect of America's demonstration of resolve on future Soviet schemes of aggression (if any). What can be said is that for the UN the longer-term consequences did not live up to the earlier optimism. Although the first moves were taken by the Security Council, the return of the Soviet Union to that body in August 1950 led the United States to attempt to transfer more of the Council's functions to the Assembly through such devices as the November 1950 'Uniting for Peace' resolution. This inevitably took the UN still further away from the role that had originally been intended for it in 1945 as an organisation that would be founded upon great power consensus. The war also sparked off an intense constitutional and legal wrangle, with the Soviet Union calling into question the validity of the Security Council resolutions on which the UN operation was based. More seriously, Moscow was infuriated by Secretary-General Trygve Lie's enthusiastic support for the UN intervention, asserting that this compromised his office. Although the United States was able to force through his re-election for a further term from 1951 to 1953, the Soviet delegation refused to have any dealings with him, making his position virtually impossible. A final legacy of the war was prolonged American hostility towards the Peoples' Republic of China: for twenty years Washington blocked the admission of the Communist government of China to the UN seat occupied by the Nationalist regime on Taiwan. It was only when the US itself made public overtures towards the Peking government in July 1971 that the US sponsored united front against the admission of the People's Republic of China finally collapsed. By a resolution of 25 October 1971, the General Assembly voted (against American opposition) to expel the Nationalists from the UN and give their place to the Communist government.

The Korean War did not mark the end of US preponderance in the UN but the ten years that followed the Korean armistice on 27 July 1953 witnessed a steady deterioration in the US power base in the organisation. This was almost entirely a consequence of decolonisation, a development which fundamentally altered the regional balance of UN membership and hence the nature of the issues that were of most concern to the General Assembly. Of the original 51 UN members, there were 20 Latin American states as against 11 Asian and only 3 African countries. Some 40 members in all could be counted as favourably disposed towards the US. The admission of 16 new African states in 1960 and a further 10 over the next four years marked a turning point which subsequent changes in UN membership only served to emphasise more strongly. Of the 152 members at the beginning of 1980, 117 were from Asia, Africa and Latin America. It may finally be noted in parenthesis that the admission of the two German states (which had been blocked while Cold War considerations left their status in doubt) on 18 September 1973 marked the effective completion of the process by which the UN became an organisation with truly universal membership.

Regional Distribution of UN Members 1945–80

	Europe	American Hemisphere	Africa	Asia (including Middle East and Australasia)	Total
1945	15	22	3	11	51
1960	28	22	25	25	100
1970	29	26	42	30	127
1980	31	30	51	40	152

Note: Numbers refer to the distribution of members at year ending.

THE DEVELOPMENT OF UN PEACEKEEPING

The creation of NATO in 1949 provided symbolic confirmation of a fact which had been plainly visible for some time: that states had ceased to rely on the UN for their security. The Korean War was the exception (more apparent than real) that proved the rule, and the last operation of its kind. However, a less central though still important role in relation to international security still remained for the UN in the form of various kinds of intervention in disputes, which have been given the generic title of 'peacekeeping' — a term that does not appear in the Charter.

One historian of the UN's peacekeeping operations has advanced an elaborate classification scheme of the range of purposes embraced by the word 'peacekeeping'.[48] Thus, the UN may become involved in 'patching up', 'prophylactic' (preventing deterioration), or 'proselytising' (promoting change) activities, and use a variety of means towards these ends: including *investigation* of disputes (as in the Indo-Pakistani conflict over Kashmir in 1965 or the Indonesian-Malayan dispute over the creation of Malaysia during 1964–5; *mediation* (as in the Dutch-Indonesian conflict, the Palestine issue, and the frictions between Cambodia and Thailand in 1962); *supervision* of agreed settlements (as in the creation of the UN Emergency Force [UNEF] following the Suez crisis of 1956 or of the UN Yemen Observation Mission [UNYOM] to observe Egyptian and Saudi disengagement from the Yemen in 1963); *administration* (as was suggested for Trieste and in 1947 for Jerusalem, or as was established on a temporary basis in West New Guinea to arrange the transfer of that territory from the Netherlands to Indonesia in 1963); *accusation* (bringing pressure to bear against a wrongdoer through various devices designed to publicise the alleged wrong, as when a UN fact-finding group was sent to Laos in 1959 to investigate incursions by North Vietnam, or when an observation group, UNOGIL, went to Lebanon in 1958 to look into claims of Egyptian interference); *sedation* (attempting to calm down a potentially dangerous situation, as when Secretary-General Dag Hammarskjöld visited the Middle East in 1956 at a time of rising tension there, or when the UN Military Observer Group for India and Pakistan, UNMOGIP, was established in 1949 to prevent incidents on their Kashmir ceasefire line from escalating into all-out war); *obstruction* (interposing a non-fighting UN force between two opposing armies in the hope of thus deterring war, as in the case of UNEF, or the UN Force in Cyprus, UNFICYP, and the UN Force in Lebanon, UNIFIL); *refrigeration* (where the UN directly administers an area to allow tempers to cool and stability to be restored, as was the initial intention behind the UN's largest peacekeeping operation, in the Congo in 1960); *invalidation* (where a UN investigation is proposed with the ulterior objective of casting doubt upon the very legitimacy of a particular regime, as was suggested by the Western powers in relation to several Soviet satellite states in the 1948–52 period); *coercion* (where more direct pressure than the moral kind involved in the invalidation process is applied to promote change, as in the case of UN economic sanctions from 1966 onwards against the Smith regime in Rhodesia).

This framework shows that the narrower conception of UN peace-keeping — the despatching of a military group to some trouble spot in order to maintain order there — is but a part of a much larger and more complex pattern of UN involvement in international security. It also places UN peacekeeping in its true historical context: as a continuation and development of earlier practices, especially in the League. Here we shall consider further the three examples of UN peacekeeping which had the greatest impact on the Organisation: the UN operations in the Middle East (especially the creation of UNEF) and in the Congo, and the imposition of economic sanctions on Rhodesia.

UNEF deserves special mention because it was the first substantial venture of its kind and because, in a sense, it was conjured out of nowhere since such a force had not been envisaged in the Charter. In 1948 Trygve Lie had proposed the creation of a small UN standing force that would be used purely for peacekeeping purposes, but, in the face of great power opposition, he revised this scheme in favour of the establishment of a more modest panel of field observers.[49] This was to support and provide security for UN missions and proved invaluable in underpinning UNEF when the latter was constituted. But it was not in itself a precursor for UNEF.

UNEF was established in November 1956, at the height of the Suez crisis, which arose from the Anglo-French intervention in the fighting between Egypt and Israel. The first contingents arrived on 15 November and the force reached its peak size of over 6000 within a few months. The force originated in a proposal by Canada's External Affairs Minister, Lester Pearson, and had three principal objectives. Its immediate aim was to stop the fighting in a potentially dangerous situation, where Security Council action had been vetoed by its two European permanent members. It was also intended to provide a face-saving pretext for Anglo-French withdrawal, since Britain and France had protested from the start that their intervention was motivated only by pure-minded concern for maintaining peace in the region. And it had the longer-term aim of establishing conditions, notably a peaceful Israeli-Egyptian border, which might facilitate an eventual settlement between the two countries. Britain, France and Israel hoped that UNEF would be a bargaining counter in negotiations with Egypt — that it would have the same political effect as their intervention had been intended to — but the General Assembly and the Secretary-General successfully resisted this.[50]

Five aspects of the UNEF experience were influential in the subsequent history of UN peacekeeping. The principle was firmly laid down that its function was not to fight but to act as a buffer between the two sides. It was established as a result of a General Assembly resolution and a major role in its creation and subsequent direction was assumed by the Secretary-General, Dag Hammarskjöld. These two features of UNEF were partly responsible for its legality being challenged by the Soviet Union, which claimed that the Charter gave sole responsibility for any UN action in the peace and security field to the Security Council.[51] Fourthly, it was decided from the outset that UNEF 'would be limited in its operations to the extent that the consent of the parties concerned is required under generally recognised international law'.[52] This principle of consent later enabled the Egyptian leader, Colonel Nasser, to demand the withdrawal of UNEF shortly before the 1967 Middle East War. Israel had throughout refused permission for UNEF to be stationed on its side of the ceasefire line and maintained this refusal in 1967, when Secretary-General U Thant, in a desperate attempt to salvage the situation, asked if the UNEF troops expelled from Egypt could resume their duties (and hence their buffer role) on the Israeli side of the line.[53] A final precedent for the future in 1956 was the decision that the permanent members of the Security Council should not be able to contribute troops to UNEF. This had the limited purpose at the time of ensuring that Britain and France could not participate, but it later became clear that such a rule had the effect of keeping possible cold war frictions out of peacekeeping operations and the principle was observed in future actions, except in

Cyprus, where Britain already had troops stationed and able to play the major part in UNFICYP.

Shortly before the 1967 Middle East War, U Thant was to claim: 'For more than ten years UNEF, acting as a buffer between the opposing forces of Israel and the United Arab Republic on the Armistice Demarcation Line in Gaza and the International Frontier in Sinai, has been the principal means of maintaining quiet in the area.'[54] A more realistic appraisal is made by Alan James, who argues that UNEF was not in itself a fundamental factor in maintaining the peace but that it merely 'helped Israel and Egypt to implement their temporary disposition to live in peace'.[55] None the less even this more limited role was valuable and at times dangerous: eighty-nine UNEF members lost their lives between 1956 and 1967.

The UN intervention in the Congo lasted from July 1960 until June 1964 and was the largest and most controversial UN operation since the Korean War.[56] A UN force (titled Operation des Nations Unies au Congo, ONUC) had been requested to deal with the anarchic situation in the Congo following its independence from Belgium in June 1960. The main elements of the Congo crisis were an army mutiny accompanied by atrocities against the remaining Belgians, the seccession of the richest province of Katanga and tribal breakaway movements elsewhere, a military intervention by Belgium to protect its nationals, and divisions in the Congolese government which to some extent reflected (and were fostered by) the intrusion of the cold war.

The Congo intervention led to a financial and constitutional crisis for the UN, largely because of opposition by some states to the way in which the mandate of ONUC was steadily expanded as the situation worsened. The Soviet Union in particular had supported the initial UN intervention (and provided logistical assistance for transporting the first UN units to the Congo), because it had seen this as providing a possible propaganda weapon against Belgium and 'Western imperialism' in general. Its interpretation of ONUC therefore was that it should merely conduct a holding operation to enable the 'aggressors' to depart and the lawful authorities to re-establish their control. But as it soon became apparent that the Congo faced the possibility of large-scale civil war and not just a temporary breakdown in law and order, so ONUC's mandate became progressively wider. A legal turning point was the Security Council resolution of 21 February 1961, following the assassination of Congolese Premier Patrice Lumumba, which gave ONUC the power to use force to prevent civil war and not, as previously, only in self-defence.[57] The Soviet Union had been prepared to support a substantial UN role in the Congo, but only on its own terms, which included the complete subservience of ONUC to the will of the pro-Soviet Lumumba.[58] But the UN involvement developed in ways that tended, if anything, to serve American interests in the Congo to the detriment of Moscow's objectives.[59] This inevitably led to several bitter Soviet attacks on ONUC, with Moscow's opposition focusing on Dag Hammarskjöld. He was accused of bowing to American pressure in his conduct of the operation and even of 'criminal activities', including complicity in the murder of Lumumba. One measure of Moscow's displeasure was its proposal that a three-man 'troika' with Western, Communist and neutral representatives should replace the existing office of Secretary-General. Moscow and France, which was at odds with the UN for other reasons, also refused to contribute towards the costs of ONUC.

At one level the UN intervention in the Congo could be counted a great success. One assessment credits it with having

brought an end to foreign intervention in the Congo, prevented the country from becoming a cold war area, preserved its unity and helped the Congolese people to develop a greater consciousness of their national identity, in addition to its remarkable though less advertised record in public administration, technical assistance, health services and education.[60]

Much of this is valid but there is also a negative side. From the start Hammarskjöld had taken the initiative in the Congo, and although many admired his firm handling of the situation, other states apart from the Soviet Union had misgivings about his conception of the Secretary-Generalship. These were increased by the tendency of some of Hammarskjöld's subordinates on the spot to interpret their powers in an ever more liberal fashion, especially after ONUC moved into Katanga.[61] After Hammarskjöld's death in an air crash in September 1961, his successors, U Thant and especially Kurt Waldheim, tended to revert to a less ambitious view of the Secretary-General's role than either Hammarskjöld or Lie had held. The financial crisis caused by the Soviet-French refusal to support the costs of ONUC also had far-reaching and long-lasting repercussions for the UN in general and peacekeeping in particular.[62] ONUC was recalled largely because of the financial crisis, the UN for a time was close to bankruptcy and the Soviet Union was threatened with the loss of its vote in the General Assembly under Article 19 of the Charter. It was also clear that the future role of UN peacekeeping would be very much more modest than it had been in the Congo.

The UN's involvement with Rhodesian affairs began in 1962 when the General Assembly declared Southern Rhodesia to be a Non-Self-Governing Territory, as defined in the Charter and against British insistence that it was in fact self-governing. Further resolutions followed calling upon Britain to take action to bring about majority rule. In November 1965 the minority government of Ian Smith issued a unilateral declaration of independence. Britain, followed by Commonwealth and OAU countries, immediately imposed a range of economic sanctions upon Rhodesia, some of which, including an embargo on oil exports to Rhodesia, were supported from the outset by the United States and France.[63] However, Britain did not ask the UN to instruct its members to impose mandatory economic sanctions under Article 41 of the Charter until December 1966. This was the first time Article 41 had been invoked. In May 1968 the Security Council voted to widen the range of sanctions against the Smith regime, and at the same time UN members were asked to aid the liberation in Rhodesia. A few additional sanctions were imposed in 1976 and 1977 to cover some remaining loopholes.

As with all such measures, which were designed to achieve their purpose indirectly over a period of time (by bringing steadily increasing pressure to bear on the Smith regime), it is not easy to assess the precise impact of sanctions. By December 1979, when Smith finally accepted a constitution based on majority rule, guerrilla violence was stretching the Rhodesian security forces to their limits. Moreover South Africa, which had shielded Rhodesia from the worst impact of sanctions, had been steadily retreating from its total commitment to white Rhodesia, especially after the 1974 *coup* in Portugal brought independence for the other bulwarks of the old order in southern Africa: Angola and Mozambique. These factors were undoubtedly of crucial importance in bringing majority rule. But the sanctions played a part in the gradual erosion of white Rhodesian self-confidence. Their impact was threefold. Firstly, they isolated Rhodesia diplomatically. This had a cumulative effect on white Rhodesian morale: at first it actually strengthened it by fostering a sense of uniting against the world in a noble cause, but fourteen years of being treated as an international pariah and being denied normal diplomatic relations eventually took their toll. This was probably the most successful aspect of the sanctions. Secondly, the UN was able to confer a degree of legitimacy on the use of violence by Rhodesia's liberation groups. Some would question the wider and longer-term implications of this: if violence, even in what was generally seen as a just cause, was made morally acceptable by the UN itself, this could weaken the UN's standing as a symbol of peace and remove one constraint on the use of violence in more dubious circumstances. Against this it could be argued that the 'just war' is a valid concept in several moral systems and a consensus at the UN is as reasonable a device for determining 'justness' in specific cases as any other means.

Thirdly, the most controversial facet of the Rhodesian sanctions was their economic effect, which, naturally, was intended to be their most important contribution to bringing down the Smith regime. As it turned out, the sanctions did cause substantial economic damage but evasion, especially in crucial areas like the supply of oil to Rhodesia, was so widespread that their impact was never decisive. Both imports and exports slumped in the early years, but later, as the means of circumventing sanctions grew more sophisticated and systematic, Rhodesia's trade recovered, albeit not completely.[64] While a major trading nation like South Africa and leading oil companies were prepared to collaborate with Rhodesia in ending sanctions, the latter could never be more than an irritant. But the considerable improvement in Rhodesia's economic performance in the year after sanctions were lifted suggests that the irritant was in some respects a serious one.

THE 'NON-POLITICAL' UN

The UN embraces a wide range of institutions which were established to serve various functional ends. Some of these, such as the International Monetary Fund (IMF) and the World Bank, effectively lead an independent existence from the mainstream of UN activities. Others are so closely attuned to the prevailing wind from the General Assembly that, far from being 'non-political' as intended, they mirror in every respect the conflicts and alignments of the Assembly. In addition to its permanent, specialised agencies, there are also numerous commissions, *ad hoc* groups, 'programmes' and 'funds'. An assessment of the functional activities of the UN as a whole is impossible in this small section. Some have been highly praised, others have been accused by the UN's own vetting system of corruption and gross incompetence, and to do justice to the causes of these differences amongst the agencies themselves would require a separate dissertation.[65] We shall confine ourselves here to considering briefly the UN's Economic and Social Council (ECOSOC) and the Educational, Scientific and Cultural Organisation (UNESCO).

ECOSOC, it will be remembered, was the eventual fruit of the Bruce Committee's proposals on expanding this side of the work of the League of Nations. It was intended to be the chief co-ordinator of the UN's economic and social activities and was given a special responsibility to promote respect for and observance of human rights and fundamental freedoms.[66] ECOSOC's subsidiary bodies include committees or commissions on natural resources, statistics, science and technology for development, human settlements, transnational corporations, social development, population, human rights, the status of women, and narcotic drugs. The Council is also nominally the supervising body of several regional commissions whose purpose is to assist in their region's economic and social development and to promote closer economic relations among the countries of the region. The present regional commissions cover Africa, Asia and the Pacific, Europe, Latin America and western Asia. Also formally under ECOSOC auspices but in practice autonomous are such bodies as the United Nations Children's Fund (UNICEF), the Office of the High Commissioner for Refugees (UNHCR), the Industrial Development Organisation (UNIDO), and the UN Development Programme (UNDP).

ECOSOC and its various subsidiaries have evolved since 1945 in line with changing needs and UN membership. The Council's discussions in its first years were dominated by the economic reconstruction of Europe and the problem of unemployment. In common with the rest of the UN, it soon found the cold war intruding on its discussions, which became marked not just by the power political conflict between the two superpowers but by profound ideological divergences over economic doctrine.[67] The general sessions of ECOSOC were increasingly used by the two superpowers to score debating points off each other, often on issues somewhat remote from the Council's primary interests. As developing countries came to dominate the General Assembly, their favoured issues of colonialism, racialism and economic inequality took up an ever-larger share of ECOSOC's agenda. The Council also found that it was unable to perform its anticipated roles of overall leadership and co-ordination of the UN's economic and social agencies.[68] This was for a number of reasons, including the Council's lack of any real budgetary control, difficulties in its own relationship with the General Assembly, and a natural assertiveness on the part of some of the bodies which ECOSOC was supposed to oversee. The future of the Council seems to be in some measure dependent upon progress made towards the Third World's demand for a new international economic order, a large part in the implementation of which would, under some proposals, fall to ECOSOC.

Of ECOSOC's subsidiary bodies, those with a relatively inexpensive technical function, such as the Statistical and Population Commissions, have probably been the most trouble-free. The UN Conference on Trade and Development (UNCTAD), which began merely as an *ad hoc* conference, albeit the largest up to that time (1964) has been highly successful in another sense: not only has it become a standing body but it has been an influential forum for Third World economic proposals. The regional commissions have steadily expanded their range of activities, and have played an important part in the establishment of regional banks and in encouraging regional trade and economic integration, as well as in a host of more specific projects. It should, however, be noted that the regional commissions have encountered rivalry from both the extra-UN regional organisations and some of the regional branches of other agencies. Whether this reflects a healthy pluralism or a wasteful diversion of resources is a matter for debate. UNICEF was created in 1946 with the original aim of providing relief to young victims of the Second World War, but has since concentrated its activities on helping children in developing countries, especially in the wake of disasters. Its revenue comes entirely from voluntary sources (over half from governments) and totalled $211 million in 1978. Since 1976 its emphasis has been the provision of basic medical, nutritional and educational services to children in the poorest countries. In 1965 it was awarded a Nobel Prize. The largest recipient of voluntary funds is UNDP, which received contributions from most UN members totalling over $680 million in 1979. It has concentrated on providing technical and pre-investment assistance and, like UNCTAD and ECOSOC in general, could expect a major expansion of its role within a new international economic order.

UNESCO was established at a London Conference in November 1945 with the objective of promoting international collaboration in education, science, culture and communications. It quickly attracted the services of some talented individuals, including Julian Huxley, Joseph Needham and J. B. Priestley.[69] In this it followed in the footsteps of its League of Nations predecessor, the International Institute for Intellectual Co-operation (IICI), with which people of the eminence of Albert Einstein and Sigmund Freud were associated. However, where the IICI had been essentially a high-level debating society without any practical application, it was soon clear that UNESCO would develop beyond this into a more inter-governmental structure.[70] This inseparability of UNESCO from the highly charged atmosphere of international politics in the cold war era meant that early ideals of a free and harmonious intellectual exchange had to be abandoned. On the other hand, with a budget of only $8 million a year in 1950, it was ineffective as an agent of reform and soon came under considerable criticism.

UNESCO did not really acquire a clear focus until the sharp increase in its African membership in 1960 threw into relief its function as a development agency and particularly its potential contribution to overcoming illiteracy in the Third World. Similarly, in its scientific work UNESCO's emphasis shifted towards such problems as the transfer of technology from rich to poor countries. Hitherto its scientific projects had covered less political matters such as oceanography, the supply of water in arid zones, plant and animal ecology, and the possible supply of energy from sources such as solar and wind power. Equally, its cultural work changed its scope to some extent away from intellectual exchanges and the preservation of monuments and historical sites, where its most famous achievement had been to save Abu Simbel and other Nubian temples from flooding by the Aswan Dam.[71] Third World nationalism took UNESCO into new (and often valuable) areas, such as researching the cultural heritage and pre-colonial history of African and other countries which lacked a written historical record. There was also a growing emphasis on criticism of 'cultural imperialism' which was a facet of the larger anti-imperialist campaign being conducted throughout the UN. UNESCO has also stretched its mandate somewhat by participating in specific political conflicts, as in 1974 when it criticised Israel for its archaeological work in Jerusalem and passed other anti-Israeli resolutions.[72]

The most controversial impact of the new states has been in the fourth of UNESCO's main fields of interest: communications. The Preamble of UNESCO's Constitution states unequivocally that its members (who did not, at first, include the Soviet Union):

believing in full and equal opportunities for education for all, in the unrestricted pursuit of objective truth, and in the free exchange of ideas and knowledge, are agreed and determined to develop and increase the means of communication between their peoples and to employ these means for the purposes of mutual understanding and a truer and more perfect knowledge of each other's lives.

Its first Article refers to 'the free flow of ideas by word and image', and for the first twenty years freedom of information was the prevailing ideology of UNESCO. However, throughout the 1970s it encountered opposition from many Third World and Eastern European countries. The developing countries were concerned that Western dominance both in the production of communications equipment and in the actual content and supply of information was leading to a situation where, as Hoggart puts it, 'the flow of material and opinions is massively one way'.[73] Solutions to this imbalance range from suggestions for a Third World news service to proposals emanating especially from the Soviet Union for government control of the mass media, with particular emphasis on preventing the use of satellites to beam unwelcome material into foreign countries.[74] This debate, which has yet to be resolved, goes to the heart of fundamental questions about the purposes and philosophy which are to guide UNESCO in the 1980s.

THE UN AND DIPLOMACY

In 1949 George Kennan wrote a characteristically perceptive memorandum to the State Department considering the UN from the perspective of traditional diplomacy.[75] He began by pointing to the lack of recognition given to inequalities of size between states in the General Assembly and the dubious validity of some states' claim to equal sovereign status, concluding that the Assembly merely represented 'a fortuitous collection of social entities which happen at this stage in human history to enjoy a wide degree of acceptance as independent states'. He went on to express doubts about the role of the Assembly as 'a new theatre of diplomatic operations':

Whereas in traditional diplomatic practice, the opinions of interested states were consulted and given recognition in slow, deliberate processes which left plenty of time for reflection and plenty of room for flexibility in the preparation of decisions, here decisions, when they come, are instantaneous and final and represent the voting attitudes taken at the crucial moment by the countries concerned. Everything is staked, for better or for worse, on that particular moment. Such measures of precaution as may be taken in advance to assure a favourable outcome on a particular issue must proceed through a highly complex system of contact with the delegates of dozens of other countries, most of them far removed, administratively and geographically from their home office.[76]

He singled out for special criticism the general declaratory resolutions popular (then as now) in the General Assembly:

There is prevalent in the United Nations milieu an illusion that the postures assumed by the Assembly in relation to various bodies of verbiage . . . are somehow the decisive events in world affairs. This turns the work of the Assembly, which should be addressed to real things, into a sort of parliamentary shadow-boxing: a competition in the striking of attitudes in which the stance is taken for the deed, and the realities are inferred rather than experienced. This is a contest of *tableaux morts*: there is a long period of preparation in relative obscurity; then the curtain is lifted; the lights go on for a brief moment; the posture of the group is recorded for posterity by the photography of voting; and whoever appears in the most graceful and impressive position has won.[77]

He concluded by expressing his misgivings about the tendency for the United States' UN delegation to see itself almost as a separate foreign office.[78]

Years later an American conservative was to write that the UN not only ignored political reality, but that the one-sided and selective moral indignation of the General Assembly had caused it to lose contact with any genuine moral basis: 'The United Nations is the most concentrated assault on moral reality in the history of free institutions and it does not do to ignore that fact or, worse to get used to it.'[79] Another charge frequently brought against the UN as a forum for diplomacy is that of irrelevance. Most important negotiations between the superpowers do not take place within the Security Council, while the Assembly is seen as a talking shop where the impotent upbraid the powerful. Even smaller states can and do pursue their quarrels, sometimes to the point of war, without any reference to the UN.

A book published in 1974 argues cogently that not only is the UN of limited value as an aid to diplomacy but that it is misleading to see it at all in this light: its role has become the reverse of that inscribed in the Charter, so that it is now an 'arena for combat' rather than an instrument of conciliation.[80]   In particular, states use the UN to embarrass other states, to publicise some alleged wrongdoing on the part of an enemy, to enhance the status of their side in a conflict, to lend an aura of international legitimacy to their actions, and to 'socialise' conflicts, or turn them into international issues. In all such cases resort by states to the UN has to be seen as a 'hostile act', and 'use of the United Nations as a battleground, like other hostile acts, contributes to the intensity of disputes and diminishes possibilities for peace'.[81]

Valid illustrations of all these charges abound. Indeed, as has been shown, it was the deliberate intention of the United States from an early stage to use the UN in pursuit of its own cold war policies, so that the later American reaction to Third World attempts to employ the UN for narrow political purposes may sound somewhat hypocritical. Since 1960, with the great increase in African membership of the UN, the UN's role as an arena for conflict has most frequently been seen in colonial and racial questions and in relation to Israel, reflecting the dominance of Third World countries in the General Assembly and the importance of the Arab states within that group. For many critics of the UN, it reached its nadir with a General Assembly resolution in 1975 declaring that Zionism was 'a form of racism and racial discrimination'.[82]   Other notable episodes include condemnation by the UN Special Committee on Decolonisation of Britain's continued possession of Gibraltar (where over 90 per cent of the population have affirmed their wish to remain British) and the United States' 'colonial relationship' with Puerto Rico, the granting of various kinds of special status to the Palestine Liberation Organisation to enable it to attend meetings of the UN's specialised agencies and the General Assembly, and a denial by General Assembly resolutions of the validity of existing international law which provides for compensation in cases of nationalisation.

There is, of course, another side to the argument. Much of the criticism of the UN reflects the perspective of the more powerful Western states (and of the more tradition-minded elements within those countries). Less powerful countries are likely to accord the UN much more importance as a means of advancing their interests and hence to appear more strident and uncompromising in pursuit of their objectives within the UN. That these objectives differ from those of the West is hardly surprising, and the UN may even be said to have performed a valuable service in enabling issues other than the perennial peace and security questions to find a place on the international agenda.[83]

Kennan's lament over the passing of the 'slow deliberate processes' of traditional diplomacy and the related rise of multilateral diplomacy is also special pleading. The use of the UN and other international organisations for the purposes of multilateral diplomacy is a consequence, not a cause, of the revolution in international relations since 1945. With the increasing interdependence amongst states, most countries have some interest in most issues and, in the case of major international questions, would be unlikely to accept treatment of the kind meted out to representatives of the smaller states at the Paris Peace Conference, who, in Winston Churchill's words, were obliged to 'loaf morosely around Paris' while their more powerful colleagues determined the future of the world.[84] This is especially true of those contemporary issues which seem to demand a multilateral solution, such as ecological control or the development of a new regime for the high seas: issues which require the co-operation of many states.

Even if it is accepted that the UN is primarily an arena for combat rather than conciliation, this may be both inevitable and in some respects desirable. For instance, the ability of the United States to achieve a cheap and public propaganda victory by embarrassing the Soviet Union with its Security Council revelations during the 1962 Cuban missiles crisis may have worked to prevent a violent outcome to that crisis. Similarly, the former British ambassador to the United Nations, Ivor Richard, has argued that during the 1974 Cyprus crisis the prospects for war would have been much greater if the UN had not provided a forum within which Greece and Turkey could pursue their argument non-violently.[85] A standing agency for multilateral diplomacy, like the UN, might also allow continuing contact between two hostile states even when other channels of communication have broken down, as was seen during the 1948–9 Berlin crisis.[86]

However, the importance of this role should not be exaggerated since there are many other possible lines of contact open to states. UN Secretaries-General like to stress the significance of the UN in general and their own office in particular in this respect.[87] There have indeed been occasions when the Secretary-General's role has been a crucial one, as in 1955, when Dag Hammarskjöld secured the release of American airmen who had been held captive in China for some years. But in a similar incident in 1980 Kurt Waldheim was unable to secure the freedom of American diplomats who had been held hostage in Iran, their eventual release being due to the mediation of a third country, Algeria, which had offered the age-old diplomatic service of 'good offices' in this crisis. One therefore has to have considerable reservations about the following claim by U Thant:

In some cases I have succeeded in building bridges or in eliminating tensions and conflicts between nations. Major examples . . . were my efforts to mediate the conflicts between Cuba and the United States in 1962 and between India and Pakistan in 1965. Some of the minor ones might be mentioned here: the conflicts between the Netherlands and Indonesia, the Philippines and Malaysia and between Egypt and Saudi Arabia. I also successfully mediated disputes between Yemen and Saudi Arabia, Spain and Equatorial Guinea, Algeria and Morocco and Morocco and Mauretania. In addition I could claim success in disputes between Nigeria and some of the African states, between Ruanda and Burundi and Thailand and Cambodia.[88]

4 The European Community

By far the most ambitious experiment in international organisation was the creation of the European Economic Community (EEC) by the Treaty of Rome on 25 March 1957. The EEC was remarkable for many reasons — its proposed supranational character, for instance — but perhaps its unlikeliest feature was its membership, six states who had a centuries-long tradition of mutual hostility. At first the achievements of the Community amongst such former enemies gave rise to hopes that it might serve as a model for integration in other regions. But eventually it became clear that the EEC's origins lay in a unique coincidence of circumstances which not only could not be repeated elsewhere but which, as their impact became diluted by time, were insufficient to sustain the urgency of the momentum towards union in Europe itself.

European unity was an ancient ideal, but no practical steps were taken to attain it until the Second World War brought Europe to the brink of ruin. A combination of five factors after the war created the conditions that made a degree of integration possible. The first was the extent of the devastation caused by the war and the response to this of a number of leading figures in Western Europe. Although at the end of the war the dominant emotion was of vengeful hostility towards Germany, there were some who looked further ahead to reconciliation with Germany in a new, federal Europe, which, in their opinion, was the only sure way of preventing another ruinous war. Perhaps the leading figure was the Frenchman, Jean Monnet, who had persuaded Churchill to advocate Anglo-French union in 1940, and whose memorandum to the French Foreign Minister, Robert Schuman, in May 1950 led to the creation of the European Coal and Steel Community.[1] Schuman himself was a key figure, as was the German Chancellor, Konrad Adenauer, while the Italian Prime Minister, Alcide de Gasperi, was influential in securing Italian support for the proposal.[2] The exiled leaders of Belgium, Luxemburg and Holland had already in 1944 announced a customs union between their countries which was finalised in 1948 and turned into the Benelux Economic Union in 1958.[3] During the war a joint declaration by various resistance movements in 1944 had proposed a European federal union.[4] In 1946 Winston Churchill had called for 'a kind of United States of Europe', and although it became clear that he did not in fact envisage anything more than a loose form of co-operation, his speech helped to popularise the European idea.[5]

The second major factor impelling Western Europe towards integration was the threat of Soviet domination either through conquest or through Moscow's influence over those Communist parties, such as the French and Italian, which seemed close to power. Moreover, not only were individual Western European nations weak in relation to the Soviet Union, but they were even less able to deal on equal terms with the United States. They were, in effect, squeezed between the two opposing superpowers with no control over their own destinies or significant voice in other major world issues. An alliance like NATO might suffice to balance Soviet power, but for Western Europe to regain its previous status in the world more radical measures would clearly be required. The Suez débâcle of 1956 was the event which conclusively demonstrated the relative impotence of the former great powers of Western Europe and gave additional impetus to the creation of the EEC, but the decline of Western Europe was obvious enough in 1945.

The third influential factor was the realisation in many quarters that the problem of Germany might only be finally resolved within the context of a united Europe. This was fully appreciated even by the resistance leaders in 1944: 'Only a Federal Union will allow the German people to participate in the life of Europe without being a danger for the rest.'[6] They actually went so far as to call for the heavy and chemical industries of Germany to be integrated into European industrial organisations so that they could no longer be used for German nationalist aims. The theme of promoting Germany's economic interdependence with the rest of Europe became commonplace after the war, with Konrad Adenauer, if anything, even more convinced of the need for it than Germany's former enemies.[7]

A fourth, and very important element in the initial steps towards European unity was the strong support given to the idea by the United States. While Washington still hoped that the wartime alliance with the Soviet Union would continue in peacetime, with their combined power being centralised in the UN Security Council, regionalist ideas in Western Europe and elsewhere were discouraged.[8] But as this early optimism evaporated after the war, Washington became increasingly persuaded of the necessity for Western European integration. By 1949 it was axiomatic that a Western European Community should be created both as a counter to Soviet power and as the best means of resolving the German problem. Moreover, it was urged by some that the

'US role in this matter should not be one of passive encouragement'.[9] Discreet American pressure on Western European nations to develop closer ties with each other was evident from January 1947, when a speech by John Foster Dulles advocated a federal Europe.[10]

The final and most immediate impetus to the formation of the Coal and Steel Community came from various economic factors. Several European federalists, including Jean Monnet, accepted the functionalist doctrine of David Mitrany that political unity amongst states depended upon the development of links at lower, mostly economic levels, and this influenced Monnet's advice to Schuman in 1950.[11] Secondly, the economic reconstruction of Europe had already obliged European states to accept a measure of economic co-operation, a tendency that was accelerated by the offer of Marshall Aid in 1947. Indeed the offer, in line with American policy at the time, had been linked to strong encouragement for European integration.[12]

The most directly relevant economic consideration arose from a developing crisis during 1948—9 over the allied dismantling of German heavy industry, including its steel-making capacity, which had been proceeding since 1945 as part of German reparations. American policy, which was increasingly dominated by apprehensions about the Soviet Union, had been gradually moving away from its initial support for the dismantling. As early as December 1947, US Congressional hostility to the dismantling had been expressed on a number of grounds, including the facts that the Soviet Union was benefiting from the removal of industrial plant and that a policy of weakening Germany economically was not appropriate in the context of the new world situation.[13] By 1949 this had become official American policy and was being urged upon a somewhat reluctant France and Britain. French resistance to the American proposals was based in part on a lingering concern about the security implications of permitting the Germans to build up their industrial strength and hence their war potential. But of more immediate significance was the high probability of an imminent over-production of steel in Western Europe. Combined with France's likely inability to compete with German steel production because of the latter's modern plant and access to cheaper coal, this could severely damage French prospects of economic recovery.[14]

Agreement on curtailing the dismantling of German industry was finally reached at a meeting in Paris in November of the Foreign Ministers of France, Britain and the United States, Robert Schuman, Ernest Bevin, and Dean Acheson. According to Acheson, Schuman argued at the time that: 'Excess steel capacity in Germany would jeopardise the success of integration in Europe. Steel capacity must be looked at from the point of view of Europe as a whole'.[15] Shortly before the meeting the West German Chancellor, Konrad Adenauer, had written to the three men requesting an end to the dismantling operation, but offering to meet French objections by participating 'in any agency whose purpose it is to exercise supervision over the possible war potential of Germany', and adding that West Germany was 'cognizant of the fact that the security problem also embraces the capacity for steel production'.[16] The Coal and Steel Community was an imaginative way of meeting both the short-term problem of excess steel production and France's longer-term fears about a German revival, while making a first step towards eventual political unity, and accomplishing all this in a form acceptable to Germany.

The Coal and Steel Community had been preceded by a number of other initiatives designed to strengthen European unity, which mostly fell short of their mark. A major reason for this failure was British reluctance to countenance more than loose consultative arrangements which in no sense involved a transfer of sovereignty to a central authority. In March 1948 the Brussels Treaty linked Britain, France and the Benelux countries in a defensive pact which was a forerunner of NATO. A month later the Organisation of European Economic Co-operation (OEEC) was established by sixteen European states as part of their attempt to meet the Marshall Aid requirements of greater European economic integration. Potentially the most important venture was the Council of Europe, set up in May 1949 with the general objectives of promoting unity in various fields and of protecting human rights. After functioning as little more than an ineffectual debating society for several years, the Council gradually began to acquire a significant role in regard to human rights.[17] But early ideas that members would 'merge certain of their sovereign rights' vanished in the face of stubborn resistance from Britain.[18]

Britain's attitude to proposals for European integration stemmed partly from its traditional policy of remaining free of European entanglements, partly from the greater emphasis it placed upon its relationship with the Commonwealth and the United States and partly from the pragmatist's disdain for anything that smacked of Utopian idealism. The most recent evidence that Britain remained as intransigent as ever on these matters had come with her resistance to the proposed European Payments Union, which was eventually set up after months of negotiations in July 1950 with the aim of promoting European monetary co-operation.[19] It may well have been British delaying tactics on this matter which finally convinced the French that moves towards European integration would have to proceed without Britain. So, when the Schuman Plan for a European Coal and Steel Community (ECSC) was announced on 9 May, it was done in a way that made it virtually certain that Britain would not feel able to participate. Bevin, to his annoyance, was not informed in advance about the Plan. More seriously, from Britain's viewpoint, although the French offered to open the negotiations over the establishment of the Community to any European state wishing to participate, their offer was conditional upon a prior acceptance of the basic principles of the Schuman Plan, including a merging of sovereignties. Bevin's counterproposal was that a ministerial meeting should first discuss 'how the scheme would operate in detail' before formal negotiations commenced.[20] The French, with some justice, saw this as a ploy to delay, if not prevent, the Plan's adoption and reiterated their insistence upon prior adherence to the Plan's objectives as the only basis upon which negotiations could take place.[21] The final British gambit, after receiving the French reply, was to repeat in public their call for a ministerial conference. If the British aim in making this public proposal in full knowledge of the fact that the French had already rejected it was to win other European states away from the French initiative, the tactic failed, and France, West Germany, Italy, the Netherlands, Belgium and Luxemburg (the Six) agreed to proceed with the scheme on the basis of the French terms. A treaty establishing the ECSC was signed on 18 April 1951 and came into force a year later.

The ECSC was the prototype for the later European Economic Community (EEC), as indeed its treaty envisaged in giving it the aim of establishing 'the foundation of a broad and independent Community among peoples long divided by conflicts; and to lay the basis of institutions capable of giving direction to their future common destiny'.[22] Its central purpose was to set up a common market for coal and steel within which all barriers to trade were to be abolished, while a common external tariff against non-members would also be introduced. These objectives were to be achieved by pre-planned stages. However it was in the institutions of the ECSC that its truly unique features were to be found. Its Court of Justice, the prototype for the same institution in the EEC, was the first international court dealing with substantial questions to have compulsory jurisdiction over a wide area. Moreover its judgements were binding upon governments, industrial enterprises and the ECSC's institutions alike. But the most unusual ECSC body was its High Authority, which combined in itself both administrative and political (decision-making) functions. Its members had the task of representing the 'general interest of the Community', and it was given considerable discretion to make ECSC policy in such important areas as determining the levy on coal and steel firms which financed the ECSC, although its powers over certain matters were circumscribed by the need to obtain approval from the ECSC's Council of Ministers. The Council itself was not originally envisaged as a body of the ECSC by Monnet and Schuman, but was included on the insistence of Belgium and Holland.[23] The Council was to act, in effect, as the guardian of state sovereignty against the adventurous supranationalism which was implied in the original conception of the High Authority.

During the first few years of the ECSC, the High Authority flexed its muscles against governments, firms and the Council alike. But when the Six encountered their first real crisis in 1958, arising out of over-production of coal, the Council successfully asserted itself over the High Authority and the crisis was met by separate national measures rather than a Community wide plan.[24]

THE EUROPEAN DEFENCE COMMUNITY

Although the ECSC thrived in the early 1950s, the conviction of Monnet and others that it would encourage a general momentum towards integration seemed for a time to have been founded on illusion. This appeared to be conclusively demonstrated by the failure of the proposed European Defence Community (EDC).

As American policy came to be more and more dominated by its preoccupation with the Soviet Union, so it increasingly saw in German rearmament the only means of restoring a power balance in Europe which would not be wholly dependent upon a massive American military commitment. But European opposition to German rearmament was such that it could only be achieved within a framework acceptable to Britain and France. The issue became more urgent with the outbreak of the Korean War, and at the end of July 1950 President Truman gave his approval to State Department proposals to push for the creation of a European or North Atlantic army into which West Germany could be enlisted.[25] A National Security Council memorandum on 9 September (NSC 82) set out more detailed proposals for an integrated European force under NATO authority.[26] These were then presented to the United States' allies by Dean Acheson. After consultation with Monnet and Schuman and in an effort to wrest the initiative from the Americans (who, in the French view, were too anxious to proceed at once to German rearmament), the French Prime Minister, René Pléven, announced on 24 October a plan for the creation of a European Defence Community. In the Pléven Plan, the EDC was to be organised broadly along the lines of the ECSC. It would have a common budget (a longstanding French theme which Washington had resisted) and a single Defence Minister under a supranational Council of Ministers and European Parliament. Most importantly, at least from the perspective of French public opinion, the formation of a European army (and hence the rearmament of Germany) would not commence until the European defence establishments had been integrated — certain to be an extremely protracted business — and the German contingents would be incorporated only at battalion strength or less.[27]

The initial American reaction to the Pléven Plan was one of strong opposition — on the grounds that it was at best militarily impracticable and at worst merely a French ploy to prevent German rearmament by linking it to impossible political conditions. Several months of intense negotiations among the allies followed, with the French government maintaining an intransigent stance, partly because of its own precarious hold on power. Eventually the French relented on some of the original parts of the Plan, notably those relating to Germany's participation, and the American attitude switched to one of enthusiastic support for the EDC, especially after the advent to power of President Eisenhower and his Secretary of State, John Foster Dulles in January 1953.

Britain refused to participate in the EDC, so it was the six members of the ECSC who agreed upon an EDC Treaty in May 1952. However, French opinion had already begun to swing against the idea and when the Treaty came before the French Assembly for ratification it was defeated, with 99 of its 319 opponents being members of the pro-Soviet Communist Party.[28]

THE TREATY OF ROME

The failure of the EDC did not wreck further progress towards European unity: in a sense it hastened it since integrationist efforts in other fields had inevitably been postponed while the EDC was being negotiated. Released from this preoccupation the advocates of European unity turned their attention to consideration of economic union. The initiative came, once again, from Monnet, who proposed a scheme for European co-operation in the development of nuclear energy, and from the Benelux countries, who already had a common market and proposed the extension of this to the whole of Western Europe.[29] Their ideas were deliberated at a conference of the Foreign Ministers of the Six at Messina in June 1955. The meeting led to a formal resolution adopting the Benelux proposals, in which the Ministers declared that they considered the moment had arrived 'to initiate a new phase on the path of constructing Europe'.[30] This, they believed, was essential 'to preserve for Europe its place in the world, to restore its influence and to improve steadily the living standard of its population'. Their specific proposals included the joint development of communications facilities, gas and electric power and atomic energy, the progressive harmonisation of national social policies and the creation of a common market, which would be realised in stages. The Foreign Ministers also appointed one of their number, the Belgian Paul-Henri Spaak, to head a committee of experts to draft detailed proposals along the lines of the Messina Resolution. The Spaak Report was presented to another meeting of the Six in May 1956. British representatives had attended some of the deliberations of the committee, but Britain at that time still perceived its interests primarily in global rather than regional terms and withdrew from the later stages of the creation of the EEC and the European Atomic Energy Community (Euratom).

The EEC, as it was established by the Treaty of Rome on 25 March 1957, was an edifice with many layers and could be comprehended in quite different ways according to the perspective of the observer. Its fundamentals were as laid down by the Spaak Report: a customs union with a common external tariff and a commitment to pursue closer integration in various economic sectors. At another level the Community looks like a brilliant feat of French diplomacy on behalf of French national interests. During the negotiations between the publication of the Spaak Report and the signing of the Treaty of Rome, France gained the Common Agricultural Policy (CAP) to satisfy her farmers, the admission of her dependent territories to associate membership, a German-financed development loan for France to invest in them, and a series of lesser safeguards and concessions to accommodate other French interests. At a third level, the EEC seemed to some an idealistic venture into the unknown: a supranational community which could steadily expand its range of operations until it embraced all the important areas of European economic, social and political life.

The Treaty of Rome declared that its first objective was to lay the foundations for an 'ever closer union'. A principal means to this end was to be a customs union, established gradually by stages during which members would progressively reduce tariffs and quotas amongst themselves while setting up a common tariff against non-members. The second cornerstone of the Treaty was what turned out to be one of its most controversial features: the CAP. However, the Treaty sets out the objectives of the CAP only in a very general way and it took years of negotiations for the full CAP to be worked out, as is discussed shortly. The third basic element in the Treaty was its emphasis on the free movement of persons, services and capital, which was in line with the general insistence in the Treaty upon encouraging competitive, free market conditions within the Community. This latter objective was also set out in a series of specific rules designed to outlaw many practices which might prevent, restrict or distort competition. These included prohibitions against dumping and, in certain circumstances, state aid to national industries. Finally, the Treaty called for a common transport policy, the harmonisation and co-ordination of economic and social policies, the setting up of a social fund to assist labour mobility, and an investment bank to contribute to the 'balanced and stable development of the common market'.

The aspect of the EEC which aroused most initial interest was the division of responsibilities and powers amongst its institutions, since this seemed to give the Community something of a supranational character. The Community has since evolved in ways which have tended to weaken this element in its decision-making processes, but as its original distribution of powers was at the heart of its first great crisis, it is necessary to consider them in detail. The EEC's institutional structure is broadly the same as that of the ECSC, with a Council of Ministers, a Commission which possesses both administrative and political functions, an Assembly, a Court of Justice and an Economic and Social Committee. Of these, the greatest controversy has surrounded the Commission and its relationship to the Council. The clear intention of the drafters of the Treaty of Rome was that the Commission should have the pivotal role in the Community. It was to be the guardian of the 'general interest' of the EEC and its members were neither to 'seek nor take instructions from any government or any other body'. It had several powers under the Treaty through which to pursue this basic purpose, including the capacity to 'formulate recommendations or deliver opinions' at any time it considered necessary, and to 'participate in the shaping of measures taken by the Council and by the Assembly'. But the principal weapon at its disposal was that it initiated all Community policies. The Council, under the terms of the Treaty, was the body which actually decided whether a particular course of action was to be adopted, thus keeping ultimate authority in the hands of the political representatives of sovereign states. But this power was qualified by the Commission's exclusive right to initiate proposals and by the Council's need to obtain a unanimous vote if it wished to amend a Commission proposal. Other decisions were taken on the basis of a qualified majority voting system in which France, Germany and Italy had four votes each, Belgium and Holland two votes and Luxemburg one, with twelve votes required for a proposal to be adopted. The Commission also possessed a range of other functions, some of which gave it the right to take certain decisions itself, and which, added to its right of initiative, gave it what some observers saw as enormous powers without any proper checks and balances.[31]

Of course it was never the intention of the EEC's creators that the Commission would reach its conclusions in Olympian isolation. It was assumed that in reality it would be constantly engaged in a process of consultation with interested parties, including the Council, so that its proposals were already based upon a degree of consensus by the time they reached the Council. In the early years, the Europeanists saw this as producing a wholly novel 'Community method' of arriving at decisions through a 'permanent dialogue' between the Commission and the Council, a method that would oblige states increasingly to view problems within a Community, rather than a narrowly national framework.[32]

The other EEC bodies attracted less interest at first than the Commission and Council. The Court of Justice was the ultimate authority on legal questions arising out of the interpretation and application of the Treaty. The Court's potential powers were considerable, as it was given jurisdiction over states, firms and the other Community organs alike, but in disputes between states the Treaty implied that a settlement should be sought through diplomatic channels or by the Commission before the matter was brought to the attention of the Court. The European Parliament was not a legislature: this function was performed by the Commission and Council. It possessed, in some degree, one of the other normal functions of domestic parliaments, the right to scrutinise the work of the Community. The Commission in particular was obliged to answer questions from the Parliament, which also had the power to dismiss the Commission as a body. Until the first direct elections to the European Parliament were held in 1979, its members were nominated. The Economic and Social Committee was given merely advisory status by the Treaty. A final body was given a more significant role: the Committee of Permanent Representatives of the member states (COREPER), consisting of senior Civil Servants, whose task under the Treaty was to prepare the work of the Council and carry out work assigned to it by the Council. It was to operate, essentially, as the intermediary between the high politics in the Council and the detailed decision-making processes elsewhere, a function which clearly gave it the potential for exercising enormous influence.[33]

THE EUROPEAN COMMUNITY IN THE 1960s

During the 1960s the Six made considerable progress towards some of their objectives, but the decade was dominated by Britain's attempts to enter the Community and by a crisis over the CAP which brought to the surface more fundamental constitutional issues. This crisis was largely responsible for placing in considerable doubt the assumption inherent in the Treaty of Rome that integration would be an inexorable evolutionary process.

The early years of the Community were marked by great (excessive as it turned out) optimism. In 1959 the Six began negotiations to extend the area of co-operation amongst them to include foreign policy. In 1960 they decided to accelerate progress towards a customs union and to allow freedom of movement for capital. The customs union and common external tariff were in fact completed in 1968: eighteen months earlier than the Treaty of Rome had stipulated. The decision to speed up the momentum of tariff cuts was taken in the context of exceptional economic growth in 1959–60, which the Commission believed would soften the impact of the acceleration.[34]

Also in 1960–1 the first steps were taken towards common EEC policies in agriculture, transport and the co-ordination of energy and social policy.[35] Not all of these initial moves were made without difficulty: the various agreements relating to the CAP were only arrived at after an arduous negotiating session that lasted from 4 December 1961 until 14 January 1962, a harbinger of future problems in this area.[36] In March 1961 a symbolic moment came when the Commission referred to the Court of Justice two complaints that Italy had infringed the Treaty of Rome. This was the first time that the Commission had brought a case of infringement before the Court and, moreover, the first occasion on which a member state had been arraigned by a Community institution.[37] Later in 1961 the Community adopted its first Regulation on the free movement of workers, while in July of the same year it signed its first Association agreement (with Greece). Under this Greece received certain trading preferences but without participating in the Community organs. Finally the Community had begun to acquire an identity as an actor on the international stage which was distinct from the individual identities of its members. Many non-member states established diplomatic relations with the Community, and when the United States from 1959 onwards began to push for a multilateral tariff-reduction conference within the framework of the General Agreement on Tariff and Trade (GATT), it was decided that the Commission would conduct negotiations in such a conference on behalf of the EEC as a whole.[38] During some of the 'Kennedy Round' talks which ensued the Commission was able to act with considerable independence.[39]

The success of the Community was such that those European states which had refrained from joining it in 1957 soon overcame their initial doubts and applied for membership. The most important of the outsiders was Britain, which had in the late 1950s tried to circumvent the trading disadvantages of non-membership by promoting a scheme for a general free-trade area between the Six and other European states who were OEEC members. But although five out of the Six were favourably disposed to this idea, the advent to power in France of General de Gaulle in June 1958 soon brought negotiations to an acrimonious end. Britain's response was to form a European Free Trade Association (EFTA) in November 1959 with Denmark, Norway, Sweden, Austria, Switzerland and Portugal.

Britain's change of heart about EEC membership, culminating in her application to join in July 1961, had come about partly because of the increasingly evident contrast between the Community's excellent economic performance and Britain's relative economic failure. But of at least equal importance in the eyes of the British Prime Minister, Harold Macmillan, were the political arguments in favour of membership.[40] Britain's 'search for a role' since the Second World War had taken it from the effective end of its empire with Indian independence in 1947 to a full realisation during the 1956 Suez crisis of how far it had fallen from great power status. It retained a sentimental attachment to its links with its former colonies in the Commonwealth, which was also a source of cheap food imports, but the main thrust of its foreign policy since 1945 had been to maintain a close relationship with the United States. But by 1960, the United States was less interested in a 'special relationship' with Britain than in the development of a strong and united Western Europe as a countervailing force to Soviet power. The EEC, with its aspirations towards economic and political unity, looked the most promising prospect for the fulfilment of this goal. Signs of American coolness towards Britain's policy of detachment from European integration had appeared with the accession to power of President Kennedy's administration in 1961.[41] When Macmillan announced Britain's application for EEC membership he stressed the economic reasons for joining, in an obvious effort to play down the sovereignty question which had been at the root of earlier British apprehensions about the Community. But he did acknowledge that Britain's application had political as well as economic motives in that it 'added to our strength in the struggle for freedom'.[42] He also set out certain conditions for British membership, notably that the interests of the Commonwealth and EFTA would be taken into account and that the standard of living of Britain's agricultural community would be safeguarded.

Protracted and involved negotiations now ensued, continuing throughout 1962. There is room for doubt as to General de Gaulle's true attitude to these negotiations. The French delegation relentlessly created obstacles, difficulties and delays over every item on the agenda, beginning with its insistence that the Six should first reach a common position on each issue before they could discuss it with Britain. This could simply have been evidence of de Gaulle's determination to safeguard French interests, which might be endangered by British entry. Equally, however, it could have been a tactic designed to make the terms demanded for British accession to the Treaty of Rome so rigorous that Britain would be provoked into withdrawing. 1962 was a difficult year for France, with disengagement from Algeria, the details of the CAP to be fought over and a general election to be contested. France's calculation may have been that the desire of its EEC partners to admit Britain could not be successfully resisted at a time when France faced so many other difficulties, so that France needed to play for time until the other problems were resolved.[43]

When de Gaulle eventually vetoed British entry at a press conference on 14 January 1963 he gave as his reason his belief that Britain, with its worldwide connections, was not yet sufficiently 'European' in its out-look for its application to be accepted. In fact his decision was almost certainly based upon some less high-minded considerations. Britain would have been a threat to French leadership within the Community, which de Gaulle saw as a precondition for France's restoration to its rightful place in the world. But an even more serious danger to his aspirations for France stemmed from the possibility that Britain might act as a kind of 'Trojan horse' for American political and economic power, which could turn the Community into a vehicle for American hegemony. De Gaulle might have thought his worst fears about the Anglo-Saxons had been confirmed when, in December 1962, Kennedy and Macmillan had met at a conference in Nassau and agreed to promote the idea of a multilateral nuclear force (MLF) which ran counter to de Gaulle's ambition for France to acquire its own independent nuclear force.[44] By January the negotiations over British entry were reaching their climax despite all obstacles the French had put in their way, so clearly the moment of decision for de Gaulle was approaching. Another reason that de Gaulle chose to speak then was that Germany, the only member of the Community with any prospect of resisting him, was unwilling to do so because of Chancellor Adenauer's desire to secure a Franco-German Treaty of Friendship, which was due to be signed later in January.

The contempt shown by de Gaulle for his Community partners (whom he did not consult about this announcement) and for the 'Community method' of making decisions on the basis of consensus caused a brief crisis, but by the middle of 1963 the EEC seemed to be safely back on course. In July the Six signed an association agreement, the Yaounde Agreement, with eighteen independent African states. During 1964 some progress was made on other matters, including greater freedom of movement for workers within the Community and co-ordination of the separate monetary policies of the Six. In April 1965 it was decided to merge the executives of the three Communities (the EEC and Euratom Commissions and the ECSC High Authority) into a single Commission.[45] But these apparent signs of the Community's health disguised fundamental differences about the EEC's nature and purposes which erupted in 1965 into its worst crisis to date.

The crisis essentially concerned French opposition to any conception of a Community with supranational authority, but it was occasioned by a dispute over the CAP, to which we must now turn. The basic objectives of the CAP were to provide a stable market for agricultural produce while ensuring that the interests of farmers in receiving a fair income and of consumers in paying reasonable prices were both met. The main elements of the CAP were agreed in principle during negotiations between 1958 and 1960, and the basic rules and regulations were decided in January 1962. The cornerstone of the policy is a market-support system under which the Community intervenes to buy up surplus agricultural produce should the price fall below a previously agreed level. Imports from outside the Community incur levies to bring them up to a 'threshold price', which ensures that they cannot undercut the prices charged by Community producers. Producers also receive export subsidies to enable them to compete on equal terms on the world market.

The CAP has encountered several problems during its existence. The most basic concerns the inescapable problem of how to intervene in a free market in such a way as not to create inefficiency and wastage: if the support price is set at too low a level, hardship to farmers is caused, but if it is too high, overproduction may occur. This latter factor was responsible for the Community's famous 'butter mountains' and 'wine lakes' of the 1970s. But in 1964–5 more pressing problems were apparent. The Six already had their own support schemes for their individual agricultural sectors, and these inevitably varied widely. A notable difficulty concerned the gap between the support prices for cereals in France and West Germany. A third major issue stemmed from the very large sums that would be needed to finance the support scheme. Although the Six were ready to incur the necessary expense, the question of how and through whom control over the financing of the CAP was to be exercised become prominent in 1965.

But during 1964 Franco-German differences over what should be the standard Community support price for cereals dominated EEC negotiations. In November 1963 the member of the Commission with responsibility for agriculture, Sicco Mansholt, had proposed a plan for accelerating the standardisation of cereals support prices.[46] For West Germany, this would have involved cutting the support price and hence antagonising German farmers just before the elections due in late 1965. Franco-German disagreements over this question became entangled with the issue of a nuclear MLF for Europe, which Bonn supported. For de Gaulle, this was fresh evidence of how the United States was furthering its hegemonic designs through its backing for proposals, like the MLF scheme, whose supposed objective was to further the cause of European integration.

Eventually, after protracted negotiations, the difficulties over cereals were resolved by a compromise package agreed in December 1964. This opened the way to the fixing of common prices for other products, but the implacable and occasionally threatening stance that had initially been assumed by the French had caused some bitterness. Hitherto a 'Community spirit' of conciliation had been supposed to prevail in negotiations amongst the Six. This notion had been severely tested in 1964 but the 1965 crisis all but destroyed it and brought to the fore fundamental differences over the very nature of the Community.

In March 1965 the Commission finalised proposals for financing the CAP through a European Agricultural Guidance and Guarantee Fund (EAGGF), to commence operations on 1 July 1967 when standardised agricultural prices were due to be introduced. However, the Commission took the opportunity of linking the EAGGF proposal to two further measures, which were designed to enhance the Community's own institutions and hence strengthen the supranational component of the EEC.[47] The first was a measure to replace the existing system of financing the Community by direct government grants by a system in which the Community would have its 'own resources' in the shape of the proceeds from levies on imports from outside the EEC and from other sources. This would add to the Commission's independence from the six governments. The second was a measure to improve the standing of the European Parliament by giving it wider powers of budgetary control. This was the most controversial of the three proposals since it would have involved an actual amendment to the Treaty of Rome. Hitherto the Parliament had had the right to propose amendments to the Community budget but there was no obligation on the Council to accept them. Under the new proposals, if the Commission approved the Assembly's amendments, the Council could reject them only if it was able to muster a five-sixths majority.

As the Commission had gone beyond its instructions from the Council in making these proposals, this was a clear and ambitious bid for an extension of the 'European' or supranational facets of the EEC at the expense of its intergovernmental elements. Given de Gaulle's well-known antipathy to any suggestion of a higher authority than the nation state, the Commission's motives in making proposals that would inevitably be highly controversial are open to question, especially as this was an uncharacteristic departure from its normal caution.[48] The Commission may simply have miscalculated the lengths to which the French would go in pressing their opposition, or it may have deliberately tried to force conflict over the supranationality issue into the open. The President of the Commission, Walter Hallstein, had long adhered to an ambitious interpretation of the Commission's functions, and his personality seems to have been an important element in pushing through the proposals against internal opposition.[49] As early as 1960, Hallstein had claimed that a proposal by the Commission was 'something more than just a compromise of the sort normally aimed at by an international secretariat; it is an autonomous political act by which the Commission, speaking with complete independence, expresses what it considers to be the general interest of the Community'.[50] He still maintained this position at the beginning of 1965, declaring that the Commission 'is the mainspring of the Community, for it alone can initiate legislation. It mediates between the Community interest and the particularist interests of the member states — and not only in the final phase of the decision making process in the Council'.[51] Moreover, he anticipated a significant increase in the Commission's powers after 1 January 1966, when a system of qualified majority voting was due to be introduced into the Council. Under the existing system the Council's business was conducted on the basis of unanimity. From 1 January 1966, in all matters that had to be passed by a qualified majority and for which the Treaty required a proposal from the Commission, at least twelve votes were needed, with unanimity required for the Commission's recommendations to be amended. In other cases, the twelve votes had to be drawn from at least four member states. The effect of this, as Hallstein was quick to point out, was that the majority twelve votes of the 'big three' would only succeed when they supported the line put forward by the Commission and one state alone would be unable to exercise a veto.[52]

It was this issue and its implications for the powers of the Commission which came to the fore when the French commenced a boycott of the EEC on 2 July 1965 after the Six had failed to reach agreement on the package of measures put forward by the Commission. De Gaulle had never been comfortable with the federalist aspirations of the EEC, and he clearly thought that the moment had arrived to challenge the irreversible slide towards supranationalism which he believed would have resulted from the package and from the introduction of majority voting. In the months that followed the French walk-out, de Gaulle spelt out his own alternative conception of Europe's future. It was, naturally enough, one which would give France a leadership role and prevent de Gaulle's worst fears of the Commission being used as an agency of American hegemony.[53] But it was also derived from an understanding of the nature of international relations which saw the sovereign state as the one true actor on the world stage, with all such supposedly supranational bodies as the Commission merely the thinly disguised instruments of states in their competition with each other. To be deceived into believing that the disguise was the reality was to sacrifice one's national interest for an illusion.

De Gaulle outlined his position at a press conference on 9 September 1965. With scant regard for historical accuracy, he declared that the Treaties establishing the three Communities had been concluded at a time of French weakness, which was why 'their main emphasis reflects the contemporary demands of the other five countries'.[54] So, inevitably, 'we were bound to take exception to France's being in pawn to a predominantly foreign technocracy . . . when the time came for us to resume full command of our nation's fortunes'. In particular, 'our sense of what is reasonable' required that no important decisions in the

Community could be taken except by governments. France was opposed to an alternative conception of Europe in which government would be 'by some sort of technocratic body of elders, stateless and answerable to no-one'.[55]

Eventually, after de Gaulle's stance had encountered serious opposition within France, and had not won over any of France's EEC partners, the Six agreed to meet in Luxemburg to try to resolve their differences. At the first meeting, on 17 and 18 January, France's Foreign Minister, Couve de Murville, presented ten proposals, whose basic aim was to place very definite limits on the power of the Commission. The main points of the document were that the Commission should consult the governments of the Six before making any proposals; that it should not reveal its proposals to the press or the European Parliament before presenting them to the Council; that the practice should cease whereby the Commission 'often proposes to the Council decisions which instead of dealing with the substance of the problems posed, merely give the Commission powers to act later but without specifying the measures which it will take if such powers are conferred upon it'; that the Commission's powers should be precisely circumscribed with no room for discretion or autonomous responsibilities; that the Council alone should have the prerogative of dealing with foreign governments and international organisations; above all, that no country should have to accept a majority decision: all Council decisions should be unanimous.

The first meeting failed to resolve the rift, but a second meeting on 28–9 January produced what has come to be known as the Luxemburg 'gentlemen's agreement'. The chief elements of this involved an instruction to the Commission to consult with the intergovernmental body COREPER before making proposals, and an agreement that where very important national interests were involved the Council would try to reach a unanimous decision.[56] The Six acknowledged a divergence of views as to what should be done in the event of a failure to reach agreement, with the French making a unilateral declaration that discussion must be continued until a consensus was formed. In fact since the Luxemburg settlement, by a tacit agreement amongst the Six, almost all Council decisions have been taken by a unanimous vote, with a consequent weakening of the Commission's original powers of initiative. In the opinion of one analyst, its proposals 'are being reduced to mere memoranda, serving only as bases for discussion instead of draft versions of laws'.[57] In essence, de Gaulle had won his point that the Community was still a collective of sovereign units rather than an embryo superstate. However, the enormous number of matters arising in the Community and the technical difficulty of many of them has necessitated a degree of flexibility in the decision-making system.

Although the Council remains the dominant body, a complex structure has grown up in which various committees of government representatives, which themselves operate on the basis of a qualified majority voting system, are attached to the Commission. Even the Council's role has been diminished by what has become a well-established practice of holding summit meetings of heads of government to determine matters of basic policy.

One unanticipated effect of de Gaulle's affirmation of state power in 1965 was that many in Britain who had originally opposed joining an apparently supranational community were converted, when it became clear that no serious sacrifice of sovereignty would be involved in British entry. A second British application to join was made on 11 May 1967, but once again de Gaulle imposed his veto in November. Progress was also blocked in other areas, such as the development of Euratom and the devising of a common technological policy, creating something of a crisis atmosphere within the Community. In its report on the activities of the Community in 1968, the Commission bewailed the effect this was having on the EEC's work: 'There has been less goodwill and conciliatory solutions have become more difficult to work out; the advocacy of purely national interests has been quite open.'[58] At the end of 1968 the second Mansholt Plan for Agriculture was produced, proposing sweeping reforms designed to rationalise farming by encouraging small farmers to leave agriculture so that larger and more productive units could be created, thus lessening the need for the inefficient protection of farmers' incomes by the CAP.[59] But in the prevailing atmosphere the time was not ripe for such a far-reaching scheme.

The situation did not improve until after de Gaulle's resignation in April 1969. Within months the Commission had recovered a little of its former vigour and begun to reiterate some of its earlier controversial proposals, such as the 'own resources' scheme and its plans for the European Parliament to have greater budgetary powers.[60] On a French proposal, a summit meeting was held at The Hague in December 1969 to discuss the development of the Community in terms of the completion of its planned phases under the Treaty of Rome, its consolidation and strengthening through additional measures such as an economic and monetary union, and its enlargement. The Hague summit reinvigorated the EEC and restored something of the 'Community spirit', although its conclusions still fell short of the Commission's more optimistic expectations. However, as The Hague summit communiqué pointed out, what had already been achieved by the EEC was considerable: 'never before have Independent States pushed their cooperation further'.[61] The communiqué went on to affirm the leaders' belief in the ultimate political objectives of the Community, to support its enlargement, to agree to a definitive financial arrangement for the CAP and to arrangements whereby the Community would be given its independent source of revenue, to propose steps towards economic and monetary union and to approve several lesser projects. Significantly it ignored the question of strengthening the Community's supranational institutions and also avoided pronouncing on proposals for direct elections to the European Parliament.

THE COMMUNITY OF THE 1970s AND 1980s

During the 1970s the EEC suffered, like the rest of the world, from the economic recession which shattered the dreams of continuous economic growth that had sustained the Community throughout the trials and tribulations of its first decade. None the less there were important developments in several areas, of which three are considered here: the enlargement of the Community, the establishment of the European Monetary System and the first direct elections to the European Parliament.

Britain, Denmark, Ireland and Norway had applied to join the Community and negotiations over the terms of entry were opened on 30 June 1970 and successfully concluded a year later. However, Norway later voted in a referendum to reject membership. In the British case, negotiations centred on Britain's financial contributions, the arrangements for her transition to the CAP, safeguards for Commonwealth exporters to Britain, especially for New Zealand and Commonwealth sugar producers, and the position of sterling in the Community's monetary system.[62] When a Labour government replaced the Conservative administration of Mr Heath, which had taken Britain into the Community, it renegotiated some of the terms and submitted the whole question of British entry to the country's first-ever referendum on 5 June 1975, which resulted in 17 million votes in favour of the EEC and 8 million against.[63]

Enlargement of the Community was certain to dilute still further its supranational features, since it inevitably introduced new factors to be taken into account in the Community's decision-making processes. This was bound to be the case since one of the new members was Britain, with its traditional wariness of things continental. Britain's economic difficulties of the 1970s did not help its adjustment to life in the Community, and several battles between Britain and its partners took place over such matters as Britain's financial contributions and the attempts to develop a common fisheries policy. By the beginning of the 1980s there was some evidence that public opinion was swinging away from its earlier support for British entry and withdrawing from the Community became official Labour Party policy.

A different kind of problem resulted from the second wave of enlargement of the Community, which began with the admission of
Greece on 14 January 1981, with Portugal and Spain expected to
follow in the next few years. All of these are poorer than the
Community's poorest member before Greek admission, Ireland, and
they have larger agricultural communities. As the President of the
Commission, Roy Jenkins, pointed out in 1979, agriculture in a Community with twelve members would account for 11 per cent of the
workforce as against 8 per cent in a Community with nine members.[64]
By 1981 some of the serious problems associated with the CAP had
lessened as agriculture within the Community had become more
efficient. The accession of Greece, Spain and Portugal could put new
strains upon the CAP. Moreover, at a time of high unemployment in
the nine most industrialised members, the principle of free movement
of labour could encounter problems.[65]

From the end of the 1960s the Western world had been troubled by
growing problems in its monetary relations, with each country's
attempts to deal with its own difficulties tending to be cancelled out by
other countries doing the same thing. None the less a summit conference
in Paris in October 1972 was still able to sound an optimistic note
about the Community's future. Its communiqué declared that economic
expansion was not an end in itself but should be used to reduce social
inequalities; it called for the first steps to be taken towards a European
system of monetary co-operation and for further improvements in the
Community's regional and social policies. The strongest emphasis was
placed on the need for co-operative approaches to the Community's
external relations, especially with regard to the problem of Third World
underdevelopment. This last was to be a recurring theme throughout
the 1970s.

But the optimism of the Paris summit soon gave way to the universal gloom which followed the oil crisis of 1973. The immediate victim
of this was the possibility of a common energy policy in the Community. Several member states, notably France and Britain, almost
instinctively resorted to dealing separately with the Arab oil producers
in an effort to safeguard their own supplies, while France opposed
attempts to produce a collective response to the crisis within the framework of the Organisation for Economic Co-operation and Development
(OECD) which included other European states as well as the United
States and Canada.[66] The change in atmosphere since the 1972 Paris
summit was reflected in the report on European union published by
the Belgian Prime Minister, Leo Tindemans, in January 1976, which
generally had a much less ambitious tone than the 1972 communiqué.
It suggested, for instance, that the nine members need not proceed at
the same speed towards the objective of economic and monetary

union. However, it did contain an echo of earlier idealism in its call
for the European Parliament to be strengthened through direct elections and by a Treaty amendment giving it powers of initiative similar
to those of the Commission.[67]

That the Community still retained some vitality was apparent from
three of its achievements in the second half of the 1970s: the Lomé
Convention with Third World countries (discussed in Chapter Six),
the European Monetary System (EMS) and the first direct elections
to the European Parliament. The EMS was agreed by the nine member
states on 5 December 1978, although Britain decided that it would not
take part in the mechanism for linking the Community exchange rates.
The System functions, in some respects, as a regional version of the
IMF. Its central element is a European Currency Unit, a unit of account
for which members exchange some of their own currency reserves,
receiving the equivalent of the IMF's Special Drawing Rights. The
essential purpose of the EMS is to reduce instability in the exchange
rates between the Community's currencies by acting as an early warning
system to detect excessive fluctuations and by enabling intervention to
support currencies under pressure.[68] To some extent the EMS has been
a success: there have been relatively few currency adjustments since its
inception despite economic and financial disparities amongst its
members. But the second stage of the EMS, which was supposed to lead
to the creation of a European Monetary Fund, was postponed when it
came up for decision in March 1981.

The European Parliament had always been the poor relation amongst
the Community's major institutions. Its formal role under the Treaty of
Rome was essentially consultative, while its only real power — its
ability to dismiss the Commission — was something of a blunt instrument since it was clearly a power which it would only exercise in conditions of extreme crisis. Its informal role in the legislative process has
been somewhat more influential than this suggests, since the Commission
is obliged to take careful account of the Parliament's views in framing
its proposals: Commission officials attend parliamentary committees,
where they have to defend and explain their proposals, and they also
reply to debates in Parliament. From this, it is obvious that the Parliament's fortunes are to some extent tied up with those of the Commission, whose role has diminished since 1965. However, the Parliament
has steadily increased its control over the Community's budget in
recent years. It now has the power to reject the budget in its entirety,
and actually did so in 1979. Moreover, it has the final say on all 'non-
obligatory' items in the total budget — a technical term which, strictly
speaking, refers to those items which do not arise directly from the
three Community Treaties but which has been used more flexibly than
this interpretation.[69] At present 'non-obligatory' items amount to

about 25 per cent of the total and the Parliament has used its powers here in 1976 to restore certain expenditures in the social and development field which the Council wished to reduce, and in 1979 to increase the Community's Regional Fund by 100 per cent, also against the Council's wishes.

The Parliament's standing, if not its formal powers, improved in 1979 when the first direct elections to the Parliament took place: the first-ever international elections. Some 111 million out of the 180 million eligible to vote did so, and they elected 410 members — an enlargement of the previous, nominated Parliament which had 198 members. It is clearly too early to assess the impact that direct elections will have. So far the Parliament has shown a tendency to want to flex its muscles against the Council, but the problem here is that the Council is still the true location of power within the Community and any significant enhancement of the Parliament's role will only take place by edict of the Council. While there is friction between the two bodies, the Council is unlikely to make concessions of this kind. None the less the Parliament remains an interesting and indeed unique institution. It is genuinely transnational, even to the point where its members sit in party political rather than national groupings. Direct elections have enabled it to claim to be the true representative of the *vox populi* of Europe, but only a general shift towards a supranational Community, which is at present unlikely, will produce a major strengthening of its role.

CONCLUSION

In 1973 the Norwegian social scientist, Johan Galtung, published a book entitled *The European Community: a Superpower in the Making*.[70] In this he considered the Community from a critical leftist perspective and found it to be, in embryo and intention, a new superpower. This conclusion derived from a comparison of the basic economic resources of the Community with those of the United States, the Soviet Union and Japan, with the Community emerging as roughly equal to the Soviet Union.[71] Its power, in his view, was being used to penetrate and dominate the Third World.[72] Eventually it would be a new capitalist superstate and the head of a system of neo-colonialism.

The allegation that the European Community is a capitalist/imperialist venture has been made by others, and to confirm or refute it would involve a detailed analysis beyond the scope of this book. On the one hand, it is certainly the case that the European Community, like other regional organisations, has attracted substantial investment funds from the large multinational corporations. It is also based unequivocally on an ideology of free enterprise. On the other hand, many Third World states welcomed the Lomé Convention (drawn up two years after Galtung's book) as a genuinely new and forward-looking approach to the relationship between rich and poor countries. But the vision of the EEC as a superstate may be briefly considered here. Galtung was unlucky in that he wrote his book in 1973, which proved to be a turning point (in an adverse sense) in the Community's fortunes because of the oil crisis. Hence predictions of giant strides towards superstatehood by 1980 have proved all too false. But even in 1973 there were clear signs that the Community was far from transforming itself into a federation with the degree of centralised authority that would be necessary for its aggregate power to amount to what Galtung already saw it as: a cohesive single force rather than a mere adding together on paper of several fragmented parts. The Community has made greater progress in international co-operation than any previous venture. It has helped to make war all but impossible in a region where it was once endemic. But despite the ambitions of some of its creators, it remains an agency for co-operation amongst sovereign states, not a means of eroding sovereignty.

5 Regional Organisation outside Europe

There is now a vast number of regional and sub-regional organisations with a range of functions embracing military, economic, political and cultural co-operation. Rather than attempting to discuss all or even many of these — a task which in one chapter would produce little more than a list of names — I will confine myself here to considering briefly the history and functions of three of the more important regional organisations, together with some of their offshoots.

THE ORGANISATION OF AMERICAN STATES (OAS)

The central fact to note about the OAS is the enormous disparity in wealth and power between one of its members, the United States, and the others. Indeed it is no exaggeration to say that the history of the OAS and more generally of regional integration in Latin America is largely identical with the history of US policies there and the Latin American response. But alongside this central theme (and to some extent an aspect of it) has emerged another: the search for a distinct Latin American identity. The OAS and other regional organisations have provided an important channel through which both themes have been expressed.

Tensions in recent years between US objectives in Latin America and Latin American aspirations for their own region may be seen as part of a more fundamental conflict between two sets of ideas about the American hemisphere, ideas which one author terms 'unilateralism' and 'multilateralism'.[1] The most famous early expression of the 'unilateralist' idea was the Monroe Doctrine of 1823, in which President Monroe declared a US special interest in the hemisphere as a whole and a determination to exclude European influence from it. In 1905 President Theodore Roosevelt added a 'corollary' to the Monroe Doctrine by which the USA asserted a right to intervene in Latin American affairs to maintain order there. At about the same time as Monroe's statement, Simon Bolivar was proposing one version of the multilateralist idea: a union of the former Spanish colonies of South America.[2] The other version of multilateralism was the concept of pan-American union (that is including the United States), which first appeared in the 1880s and which was the origin of the present-day OAS.

Pan-Americanism was first promoted by the United States at the First International Conference of American States in 1889, whose aims were to discuss and recommend:

some plan of arbitration for the settlement of disagreements and disputes that may hereafter arise between them, and for considering questions relating to the improvement of business intercourse and means of direct communication . . . and to encourage such reciprocal relations as will be beneficial to all and secure more extensive markets for the products of each of said countries.[3]

As this makes plain, the primary objective of the Conference — and the chief US interest in calling it — was the development of economic relations amongst the countries involved. This was also the aim of the first regional organisation to be established, the International Union of American States (1890), whose purpose was to collect and disseminate commercial information.[4]

Despite some marginal changes over the next forty years, including the first steps towards a system for the peaceful settlement of disputes through arbitration and other means, the organisation remained, in effect, what its name suggests: a typical nineteenth-century international union with strictly limited functions. Its four- or five-yearly conferences did, however, provide a forum for the expression of Latin American opposition to the US assumption of a general right of intervention in Latin American affairs: a right implicit in the Monroe Doctrine but which was becoming more of a live issue with the growth of US power. So great was the pressure from its neighbours that at two pan-American conferences in 1933 and 1936, the United States formally accepted the principle of non-intervention between states.[5] A period of substantial co-operation followed, which reached a peak during the Second World War, and the desire to continue this after the war gave a major impetus to the formation of the OAS.[6] The Latin American countries were also anxious to place their special relationship with the United States on a distinctive institutional basis in order to prevent that relationship from being subordinated to America's global interests in the newly formed UN. It was to a great extent the efforts of the Latin American states at the San Francisco Conference which resulted in Articles 51, 52 and 53 of the UN Charter, encouraging regional organisations to have a substantial role in the settlement of local disputes.

The OAS rests on three treaties. The Inter-American Treaty of Reciprocal Assistance (the Rio Treaty), signed on 2 September 1947, is both an alliance and a collective security pact: it provides for co-operation against aggression from outside as well as by any of its signatories. It also reflects a growing concern with what were seen as Communist techniques of subversion by referring to 'aggression which is not an armed attack'.[7] The OAS Charter, agreed at a conference in Bogota, Colombia, between 30 March and 2 May 1948, set out the Constitution of the new organisation. The American Treaty on Pacific Settlement (Pact of Bogota), agreed at the same time, provided for an extensive system for the pacific settlement of disputes, but this has had little subsequent impact.

The OAS Charter reflects the varied concerns of its members. For example, the principle of non-intervention is firmly enshrined in Articles 15 to 20.[8] These prohibit not only military intervention but 'any other form of interference or attempted threat against the personality of the State or against its political, economic and cultural elements'. This is a clear, albeit indirect, statement of the widespread Latin American fear of becoming dependencies of the United States in ways other than the normal political ones. Equally, however, US concerns are reflected in various affirmations of the principles of representative democracy and individual liberty. In other respects the Charter is a sweeping proclamation of a great range of supposedly shared values and beliefs which are virtually meaningless as guides to action — the statements, for instance, that 'the education of peoples should be directed towards justice, freedom and peace', or that 'the spiritual unity of the continent is based on respect for the cultural values of the American countries and requires their close co-operation for the high purpose of civilisation'.

The OAS has had a troubled history from the outset. A primary reason for this was what many Latin American states perceived to be Washington's use of the Organisation to pursue its cold war with the Soviet Union and especially to legitimise US interventions against left-wing regimes in the region. This issue has clouded what in some respects has been a modestly successful OAS experience in peacekeeping. A second source of dissension has been divergent US and Latin American views about the OAS role in relation to economic development and the growing tendency for Latin American countries to align themselves with the Third World in questions of international economic relations. A third problem has been the increasingly apparent deficiencies of the OAS Charter, a matter only partly resolved by revisions of the Charter in 1967, which came into force in 1970.

The first major intervention came in 1954, when the leftist government of Guatemala, which had expropriated land owned by an American company, was overthrown by an invading force of exiles who apparently enjoyed the support of the United States as well as Guatemala's neighbours, Honduras and Nicaragua. Washington had

earlier called for united Latin American action against what it termed
a 'bridgehead of international communism'.[9] The United States was
able to prevent the UN from taking up the issue by arguing that, as an
essentially regional matter, it should be left to the OAS to deal with,
a claim resented by several Latin American states because it seemed to
deny them some of the benefits of UN membership.[10] The Guatemalan
case foreshadowed what was to be a lengthy OAS involvement with the
affairs of Castro's Cuba. The United States had been unable to obtain
support from other American countries for a joint intervention against
the Cuban government, but in January 1962 it secured OAS agreement
to economic sanctions against Cuba for the latter's activities in support
of guerrillas in Venezuela. The OAS also declared that 'adherence by
any member of the OAS to Marxism-Leninism is incompatible with
the Inter-American system', and that 'this incompatibility excludes the
present government of Cuba from participation in the Inter-American
system'.[11] Further diplomatic and economic sanctions were voted
against Cuba in 1964 and 1967, although several OAS members did not
vote for sanctions and Mexico refused to impose them. Following the
example of Dr Allende's Marxist government in Chile in 1970, a
number of Latin American states re-established relations with Cuba and
in 1975 the sanctions were formally ended.

Washington's determination to prevent another Cuban-style government from emerging in Latin America was primarily responsible for its
intervention in the Dominican Republic in 1965, for which it sought
OAS endorsement. The OAS had earlier become involved in Dominican
affairs during the much-hated dictatorship of Trujillo in 1960, when,
after an OAS investigation into Venezuelan charges of Dominican
interference in Venezuelan politics, it was decided to impose economic
and diplomatic sanctions against the Dominican Republic. Partly as a
consequence of OAS sanctions, Trujillo was overthrown and a period
of instability ensued. The US intervention came in April 1965 when a
revolutionary group seemed likely to gain control of the government.[12]
The OAS as such was not consulted, and its first efforts were directed
towards bringing about a ceasefire, with many OAS members highly
critical of what they saw as an outright US intervention in the
Dominican Republic's domestic affairs. However, a majority agreed to
Washington's request that an inter-American peace force be set up to
take over the US role in the Dominican Republic. From the US perspective, this would lend a degree of legitimacy, if not respectability, to its
operation, and although some Latin American states refused to approve
the peace force for this reason, others clearly hoped that it might at
least set some constraints on the United States. But there was little
support for the US proposal that a permanent peace force be established
with the capacity for dealing with similar eventualities in the future.[13]

In disputes where the cold war did not play a crucial part, the OAS proved to be a useful instrument for effecting a peaceful settlement. It has employed the full range of techniques available to international organisations for this purpose, including fact-finding missions, behind-the-scenes diplomacy by the OAS Secretary-General, mediation, diplomatic pressure and, in the 1960 Dominican case, economic sanctions. Disputes where the OAS has helped to reduce tension include conflicts between Costa Rica and Nicaragua (1948–9), the Dominican Republic and Haiti (1949–50), Cuba and Guatemala (1950), Costa Rica and Nicaragua (1955–6), Honduras and Nicaragua (1957), Panama and Cuba (1959), the Dominican Republic and Haiti (1963–5), El Salvador and Honduras (1969), and Costa Rica and Nicaragua (1977).[14] Several of the earlier disputes were resolved partly through the efforts of the Inter-American Peace Committee, which had been created by the OAS for this purpose, but in 1956 the powers of this body were severely curtailed when it was decided that it could not send an investigative mission to the location of a dispute unless both sides invited it to do so. Without decrying what has undoubtedly been a useful role, it may also be observed that, as with other successful exercises in peacekeeping, success has been greatest where the OAS was offering, in essence, a way out with the minimum loss of face for two sides which did not really wish to raise the level of hostility between them.

A further cause for Latin American discontent with the OAS has been its relative ineffectiveness in helping to promote economic development, with some even fearing that it has instead been an instrument of US economic domination. This was especially so in the immediate postwar years, when the Latin American states failed to achieve their main aim of persuading the United States to introduce a Marshall Plan for the region. It was not until clear signs of Latin American restlessness appeared in the late 1950s that the United States moved to expand the economic role of the OAS by creating an Inter-American Development Bank, whose cumulative net lending is now well over 10 billion dollars.[15] This first step was followed by the launching of President Kennedy's Alliance for Progress in 1961. The Alliance for Progress was an ambitious and wide-ranging two-year programme, whose objectives included not only accelerated economic growth in Latin America but internal political, social and economic reforms. Perhaps inevitably such ambitious aims proved impossible to attain, although there is general agreement that the Alliance and the OAS in general performed a useful service in providing some economic aid and technical assistance and also in co-ordinating economic planning in Latin America. However, the opposing viewpoint is that the Alliance for Progress was merely another device to enable the United States to pursue policies of economic neo-colonialism in Latin America. It was certainly the case that Washington linked its aid programmes under the Alliance for Progress to its general anti-Communist policies in the region. In the United States itself another ground for opposition to allocating a larger economic role to the OAS was that this would merely entail a wasteful duplication of work already being carried out by UN agencies.

Although the most optimistic aims of the early 1960s failed to materialise, there were some steady, if unspectacular, achievements in certain areas. One was in the field of technology transfer: an important aspect of the wider demands from the Third World for a New International Economic Order. The OAS decided in 1967 to embark upon a major programme to promote the transfer of technology to Latin America. An evaluation of this programme ten years later found that, despite various shortcomings, genuine progress had been made in this field and a foundation had been laid down on which it was possible to build further.[16]

None the less, the Latin American countries have expressed a growing sense of dissatisfaction with the economic work of the OAS. This was one of the factors which underlay the 1967 revisions of the OAS Charter. These raised the status of the OAS Economic and Social Council and incorporated as an ultimate objective the economic integration of Latin America. They also replaced one of the OAS bodies, the virtually moribund Inter-American Conference, with a General Assembly, which was to meet annually and whose powers were to be enhanced.

These amendments came into force in 1970, but by then they had already been overtaken by the rapidly changing climate of international opinion. In particular the Latin American countries increasingly saw themselves as part of a Third World that was engaged in a fundamental confrontation over international economic matters with the industrialised countries, at whose head stood the United States. During the 1970s the Latin American states proposed sweeping changes in the OAS Charter, by which it would enunciate the principle of 'collective economic security' with sanctions against 'economic aggression'.[17] Understandably, perhaps, Washington has resisted these demands.

Disillusionment with what they have achieved in association with the United States has caused many to return to the older ideal of an exclusively Latin American unity, although the emphasis of all postwar schemes for regional integration has been primarily economic rather than political: a reversal of the earlier proposals. The other Latin American organisations operate at both the regional and sub-regional levels and their aims have varied in line with the evolution of political and economic philosophies over three decades.

The Organisation of Central American States (ODECA) was established by the Charter of San Salvador in October 1951 (revised in December 1962) between Costa Rica, El Salvador, Guatemala, Honduras and Nicaragua. Its purpose was stated to be the formation of an 'economic-political' community.[18] ODECA was followed in December 1960 by the creation of a Central American Common Market (CACM), which aimed to establish a customs union in the short term, and in the long term to unify the economies of its members and jointly promote the development of Central America. There are also several other special agreements and institutions linking the Central American countries.[19]

The Central American experiment has enjoyed only a limited success. It led to a massive growth in intra-regional trade in the earlier years, although this fell off later.[20] There was also a significant increase in industrial production and investment, although the vital agricultural sector was much less affected by the union.[21] A severe blow came in 1969 with the short but bitter war between El Salvador and Honduras, but this was in some ways merely a symptom of more deep-seated problems. Most notable was the fact that the two poorest countries, Honduras and Nicaragua, gained less than the others, causing much dissension.[22] An unexpected paradox was encountered during the 1960s when it became apparent that a union set up in part to liberate its members from foreign economic domination had actually succeeded in attracting greater foreign investment. Finally, schemes for integrating the five economies were found to require what was for some an unacceptable level of state intervention in economic activities.[23] Increasing revolutionary violence in the region at the start of the 1980s has introduced a further element of uncertainty.

The Latin American Free Trade Association (LAFTA) was established in February 1960 by Argentina, Brazil, Chile, Mexico, Peru and Uruguay, with Bolivia, Colombia, Ecuador, Paraguay and Venezuela joining later. Its goal is the achievement of a free-trade area through the progressive reduction of tariffs and other restrictions on trade. In practice LAFTA has proved an even greater disappointment than CACM. Intra-regional trade grew after its establishment but only to around 10 per cent of the region's total trade. As with CACM, unexpected beneficiaries were foreign investors and the much-feared multinational corporations, who were better placed than indigenous industries to exploit the opportunities provided by a larger market.[24] It also had in common with CACM the apparently inequitable distribution of benefits amongst richer and poorer members.

The Andean Group was established in May 1969 by the Cartagena Agreement, as a direct response to LAFTA's inadequacies, by Bolivia, Chile, Colombia and Peru, with Venezuela joining in 1973 and assuming something of a leadership role.[25] Its underlying philosophy represents a break with earlier Latin American projects and with the liberal economic assumptions of the European Community.[26] Its stated aims include a reduction of economic inequalities amongst its members, with preferential treatment for Bolivia and Ecuador actually specified in the Agreement. One author describes its basic ideology as one of 'developmental nationalism', with individual countries allocated a virtual regional monopoly in the production of certain industrial goods, rather than the pursuit of industrial development through the creation of region-wide enterprises.[27] Moreover, the programme is marked by a much stronger element of central planning than previous regionalist endeavours.[28] The Group has also attempted to develop an imaginative response to the problems posed by foreign investment, by which the necessary foreign capital would not be frightened away but its worst features, such as foreign domination of the national economy, might be prevented. This, however, was one of the factors behind a crisis in the Group during 1975–6 which led to the withdrawal of Chile, partly on the grounds that the investment code was too restrictive.[29] Before the crisis the Group had achieved substantial increases in trade, although its industrial development programme was already lagging behind the earlier optimistic projections. In recent years longstanding bilateral conflicts between members have come to the fore. Yet the Group continues to exist with, as one writer puts it, 'one less member but with a potentially more viable programme capable of surmounting the ideological divisions between free traders and central planners and the political frictions which have impeded all types of co-operation'.[30]

The most recent regional organisation is the Latin American Economic System (SELA), formed in 1975 with the aims of enhancing the bargaining strength of Latin America in various international fora and of jointly defending Latin American interests in international trade. It includes Cuba and the English-speaking Caribbean states, so it encompasses the whole of Latin America, although its impact to date has not been as great as was hoped.

THE ORGANISATION OF AFRICAN UNITY

As with most international organisations, the OAU was both the culmination of developments over many years and the product of a series of political bargains struck at its inception. Pan-Africanism, the idea of a United States of Africa as an ultimate aspiration, goes back to the beginning of this century[31] and became a dominating theme for several African leaders, notably Kwame Nkrumah of Ghana, which became in 1957 the first African state to gain its independence in the postwar period. However, pre-independence support for the ideal of pan-

Africanism soon evaporated amongst leaders of newly sovereign states whose first concern was with the preservation of that sovereignty. Moreover, it was increasingly apparent that what had seemed strong bonds among Africans fighting the common enemy of colonialism were less effective in forging unity after independence. Divisions emerged between Anglophone and Francophone states, between radicals and moderates, and between neighbours now able to dispute what treaties drawn up amongst Europeans had allocated them as borders. Finally, the tensions caused by the outbreak of the Congo crisis in 1960 seemed for a time to push African states into various sub-regional groupings rather than a single all-embracing entity. During 1961 and 1962, three such groupings were created, known as the Casablanca, Brazzaville and Monrovia groups.[32] Such was the reality confronting the pan-African ideal when a summit conference of all thirty-one independent African states was held at Addis Ababa in May 1963 to prepare a Charter for an Africa-wide international organisation.

Nkrumah's dreams of a superstate with its own army, parliament and government had been outlined at an earlier Foreign Ministers' conference,[33] but a more pragmatic conception of a loose association of sovereign authorities won the day, with only a token bow to pan-Africanism. Ethiopia was prominent in advocating this more modest scheme, but it was widely supported at the conference. The radicals who had pressed the case for African unity were partly appeased by a clear affirmation in the OAU Charter of support for the liberation of southern Africa: another of their cherished goals.[34]

The OAU differs from other regional organisations in that its principal aims are neither collective security nor the pursuit of economic integration. However, the OAU was given from the outset another of the classic functions of international organisations: the peaceful settlement of disputes. Its role in this regard was referred to briefly in Article 19 of the Charter and set out in more detail in a Protocol of 21 July 1964 (amended in September 1970). This established a Commission of Mediation, Conciliation and Arbitration, although as it turned out much of the OAU's peaceful settlement work was done through informal or *ad hoc* means. But, notwithstanding its possession of this function, the OAU was essentially seen as the embodiment of certain principles and, in a vague way, as the expression of an African identity, rather than as the means of achieving certain specific goals. Its principles are set out in Article 3 of the Charter:

1. The sovereign equality of all Member States.
2. Non-interference in the internal affairs of States.
3. Respect for the sovereignty and territorial integrity of each State and for its inalienable right to independent existence.

4. Peaceful settlement of disputes by negotiation, mediation, conciliation or arbitration.
5. Unreserved condemnation, in all its forms, of political assassination as well as of subversive activities on the part of neighbouring States or any other States.
6. Absolute dedication to the total emancipation of the African territories which are still dependent.
7. Affirmation of a policy of non-alignment with regard to all blocs.[35]

Within a few years an inherent clash was revealed between the principles of territorial integrity and the right of independence, with the latter cited by breakaway movements within African states. The most serious illustration of this came with the 1967–70 Nigerian Civil War, when the breakaway state of Biafra was actually recognised by several African states. Since all African states were located within artificial borders, determined to suit the interests of the colonial powers rather than any natural tribal or ethnic division, this was an issue with potentially disastrous implications throughout Africa. Not unnaturally the OAU adhered throughout the Civil War to a doctrine it had earlier agreed at a Cairo summit conference in July 1964: that 'the borders of African states on the day of their independence constitute a tangible reality'.[36]

The principal institutions of the OAU are an Assembly of Heads of State and Government, meeting at least annually, a Council of Ministers and a General Secretariat. Although there were moves by a few representatives at the Addis Ababa conference to give the Secretariat more than purely administrative functions, these were strongly resisted by the majority.[37] Various specialised commissions were also established which, after a reorganisation in 1967, included an Economic and Social Commission, an Educational, Cultural, Scientific and Health Commission and a Defence Commission. In 1968 a Bureau for the Placement and Education of African Refugees was added to these. The commissions were to have little impact, although to some extent they, like the OAU in general, acted as fora where ideas and policies could be given a preliminary ventilation prior to their re-emergence at the UN.

Measured by the yardstick of concrete achievement, the OAU would probably be judged a failure. Yet it has survived and in some respects grown, something which can only be explained by examining the role that the OAU has played both in diplomacy amongst African states and in Africa's relations with the rest of the world. Two main facets of its work will be used here to illustrate these themes: its involvement in the peaceful settlement of disputes and its role in the liberation of southern Africa.

The OAU was almost immediately faced with a potentially serious conflict between two of its members: Algeria and Morocco.[38] This involved a typical border problem bequeathed from the colonial past, complicated by the economic importance of the disputed region and ideological tensions between the leftist government of Algeria and the conservative Moroccans. An important precedent was set when a dispute between the two sides over whether the issue should go before the UN or OAU was resolved in favour of the OAU. It should be noted, however, that this was decided partly as a result of pressure from France and the United States, who wished the matter to be settled within an African context, rather than at the UN where it would inevitably become entangled in cold war politics. The OAU set up a special committee of mediation in November 1963, and in 1964 the two sides announced a ceasefire, with a settlement eventually being arrived at in 1968. This peaceful outcome was hailed by some as a great achievement on the part of the OAU, although it owed at least as much to the determination of the major powers not to become involved and of the two disputants not to let the matter get out of hand. None the less, the OAU had played a useful, if undramatic, role as an intermediary and by its consistent reiteration that borders inherited from the colonial period were inviolable.

Other conflicts were to prove more intractable. For instance, in 1964 serious fighting broke out between Ethiopia and Somalia over Somalia's irredentist claims in Ethiopia. Although there have from time to time been periods of truce in this conflict, occasionally arranged through OAU auspices, this conflict has persisted to the present day, and indeed has intensified. This dispute was to confirm what the Congo crisis had already made clear: that the OAU was powerless to prevent great power involvement in a conflict if the powers were determined to intervene. An equally bitter conflict developed between Rwanda and Burundi, where refugees from both sides were accused of subversive activities across the border, leading to frequent military clashes between the two countries. This, too, was a classic post-colonial situation, resulting from borders which cut across tribal areas, and here again the OAU could do little other than organise temporary ceasefires.[39] Similarly, the long-running feud between Uganda and Tanzania following Idi Amin's *coup* in Uganda was not finally resolved until Tanzania was provoked into invading Uganda and overthrowing Amin, thereby violating several cherished OAU principles.

A few disputes were resolved through OAU mediation. In 1972 a quarrel between Gabon and Equatorial Guinea over the ownership of certain islands was settled after both sides accepted the appointment of an OAU commission to define the maritime border.[40] The OAU was similarly useful in 1964 in assisting President Nyerere of Tanzania to end his embarrassing dependence on troops from the former colonial power, Britain, which had been called in to quash an army revolt. However, this was an unusual example of a case where the OAU was able to aid in the resolution of an internal conflict. In general, the OAU was not encouraged to intervene in the internal affairs of its members and since these, rather than inter-state disputes, produced the most serious situations of the OAU's first fifteen years, the OAU was inevitably precluded from involvement in many of the major crises. Thus, hundreds of thousands of lives were lost in Uganda, Sudan and Burundi, with the OAU barely able even to comment. But in some respects the OAU was presented with an even more difficult problem in the Nigerian Civil War because here the OAU itself became a factor, albeit a minor one, in the conflict.[41] Initially the federal government of Nigeria was adamant in refusing to permit the OAU even to discuss the war because it felt this might go some way towards legitimising Biafra as an independent entity, while the Biafran leadership was equally intent upon encouraging OAU involvement. But here too many thousands were being killed and the crisis was receiving worldwide press attention, so the OAU would have laid itself open to considerable ridicule if it had simply ignored the Nigerian situation. In the event, it established a Consultative Committee on Nigeria, but this, in line with general OAU policy, declared after its first visit to Nigeria that 'any solution of the Nigerian crisis must be in the context of preserving the unity and territorial integrity of Nigeria'.[42] Hence, because of its adherence to the territorial integrity principle, the OAU was put in the position of having to support one side in the Civil War, which inevitably damaged its chances of mediating. By 1969 the Biafran leader, Colonel Ojukwu, refused to accept any OAU role, while the federal government, in contrast, insisted that it would only accept mediation from the OAU.[43]

The other major issue which has concerned the OAU from its inception has been the liberation of the remaining African countries governed by white minority regimes, mainly in southern Africa. This has been the primary concern of the OAU Liberation Committee, which was set up at the same time as the OAU itself in 1963. The tasks of the Committee, as outlined in 1963, were to bring pressure on the colonial powers, to provide moral and material support for the liberation movements, and to act diplomatically both to secure international legitimation of armed struggle in the UN and elsewhere and to isolate the minority regimes.[44] It was also to work to unify the separate liberation movements in each country.

Only South Africa remains of the original white-dominated countries, so the liberation movement as such has clearly succeeded. This has primarily been due to armed struggle in the Portuguese colonies and Rhodesia, the collapse of the pro-colonial regime in Portugal and the

subsequent shift in South African thinking away from its total commitment to the white Rhodesian cause. But the OAU has played a
significant, if limited, role. To a considerable extent it has shaped the
response of those external powers who supported the liberation
struggles or who wished to give humanitarian aid by indicating to them
which struggles and movements it regarded as legitimate.[45] It has
helped to co-ordinate the activities of those states which allowed their
territories to be used as bases by the guerrilla movements, although it
was unable to agree upon measures to aid these states when they came
under military attack from the white regimes. It has also succceeded in
making the cause of the liberation of southern Africa an international
issue by repeated pressure at the UN. Finally, a committee of military
experts established in September 1967 proved to be a valuable source
of technical advice on fighting a guerrilla war.[46] However, in one
important respect the OAU had little success. Despite bringing very
strong pressure to bear it was unable to unify the different liberation
groups for any length of time. Its attempts in the face of this failure to
single out individual groups for its recognition as the legitimate revolutionary forces often brought more confusion than clarity.[47]

A mark of its failure in this respect is the bitter divisions and in some
cases continued fighting that still persist in some of the former colonies,
especially Angola and Zimbabwe (formerly Rhodesia). It should also be
noted that many African states have been less than willing to back their
verbal militancy in OAU debates with material assistance: the
Liberation Committee has consistently been short of funds. There has
also been a noticeable lack of unity whenever the OAU has called upon
its members to take some concrete action. For instance, after an OAU
Council of Ministers meeting in 1965 (following Ian Smith's Unilateral
Declaration of Independence in Rhodesia) called upon members to
break off diplomatic relations with Britain should the latter not use
force to end the Smith regime, only ten African states did so. Moreover,
different African states have supported different wings of the liberation
movement, which was hardly likely to assist the OAU in its avowed aim
of seeking to unite the different groups.[48]

In many respects, the OAU's most important function, both with
regard to the liberation movements and in other matters, has been to
provide one stable reference point for foreign countries in their
attempts to formulate policies towards an Africa where governments
could be replaced overnight by military or other regimes with opposite
political persuasions. It would not have been difficult for an external
power seeking influence to sponsor breakaway movements following
the Biafran example. That this has not happened to any great extent
is at least in part because the OAU has been able to present a united
front in favour of the territorial *status quo*. This has also meant that

several African states have refrained from pressing what in some respects might have seemed reasonable claims for territorial revisions along tribal lines. In a similar vein, the OAU played a significant part in important negotiations that led to a new economic relationship with the European Community.[49]

For these reasons an assessment of the OAU and the reasons for its continuing existence should not be confined to a search for specific, concrete achievements in any field. In many areas, notably the economic, social, scientific and cultural spheres, the OAU has little or nothing to show for nearly twenty years of existence.[50] Its importance lies in less tangible factors, as is suggested by one writer: 'The OAU has functioned as a neutral meeting site, an agent for interstate communications, a forum for expressing widely held opinions and as an agent able to disperse legitimisation for policy decisions'.[51] Africa's problems of desperate poverty, ethnic and tribal conflict, corruption, unstable and dictatorial leadership, and continuing interference by major powers from both east and west will not be resolved by the OAU. But without some such institution, Africa would be in danger of losing even the flimsy foundation of unity that exists over certain basic principles and with regard to such important contemporary issues as the development of a new international economic order.

As with Latin America, several sub-regional organisations have been created in Africa, but so far these have generally had a troubled history with some outright failures and no clear-cut successes. The East African Community, established as a common market in 1967, collapsed after a promising start under the weight of discord amongst its members following Idi Amin's accession to power. Similar problems have beset the Central African Customs and Economic Union (established in 1964) and the Common African, Malagasy and Mauritian Organisation (1966). There are also many smaller groupings of states, usually with more limited objectives, and these have had varying results. But the most recent addition to the list of sub-regional organisations is in some ways the most ambitious and may have the greatest prospects for success. This is the Economic Community of West African States (ECOWAS), established by the Treaty of Lagos in May 1975. The Community is the culmination of nearly fifteen years of discussion and partial and preliminary steps towards integration, promoted in the main by its largest member, Nigeria.[52] This lengthy gestation process is one reason why ECOWAS may have a brighter future than some of the more hastily formed associations of the 1960s. The other reason is the economic power of Nigeria, although this factor could work both ways, depending on the extent to which it attracts or intimidates the other members.

ECOWAS breaks through one longstanding barrier to African unity, the division between Francophone and Anglophone states in bringing together fifteen countries from both wings (as well as one former Portuguese colony, Guinea-Bissau). It has the standard bodies, including an 'Authority' of heads of state and government, a Council of Ministers, a Secretariat and a Tribunal to settle disputes. Its objectives, as set out in Article 2 of the Treaty are:

to promote co-operation and development in all fields of economic activity, particularly in the fields of industry, transport, telecommunications, energy, agriculture, natural resources, commerce, monetary and financial questions and in social and cultural matters for the purpose of raising the standard of living of its peoples, of increasing and maintaining economic stability, of fostering closer relations among its members and of contributing to the progress and development of the African continent.[53]

As with the European Community, progress towards integration and harmonisation of the national economies is to take place by carefully thought out stages, with the ultimate aim of 'the creation of a homogenous society, leading to the unity of the countries of West Africa by the elimination of all types of obstacles to the free movement of goods, capital and persons'.[54] It remains to be seen whether ECOWAS will enjoy a better fate than some of its predecessors elsewhere in Africa, but with Nigeria's oil wealth, and a combined population of 124 million people, its potential to become an important political and economic force within and eventually outside Africa is considerable.

THE ASSOCIATION OF SOUTH-EAST ASIAN NATIONS

The overall political situation in south-east Asia altered drastically during the 1960s and 1970s, far more than in Latin America or even Africa. The Association of South-east Asian Nations (ASEAN) was established in 1967 as a response to the changing circumstances of that period and its history has so far been one of bending with the prevailing winds in an attempt to protect the interests of its members. It was intended to be primarily a diplomatic tool with the emphasis on informal consultation but with the flexibility to serve other purposes when required.

Asian regionalism in the 1950s was largely confined to such economic co-operation as took place under the auspices of the UN's Economic Commission for Asia and the Far East (ECAFE) and, for Pakistan, Thailand and the Philippines, a strategic alliance with the United States and other Western powers in the form of the South-east Asia Treaty Organisation (SEATO) in 1954. The first moves towards an exclusively south-east Asian grouping came in July 1961 with the formation of the Association of South-east Asia (ASA) between the Philippines, Thailand and Malaysia. This had the aim of promoting economic and cultural co-operation through schemes for student exchange, joint shipping and airlines and the like, but a major rift between Malaysia and the Philippines and various practical difficulties prevented any real progress from being made.[55]

Four factors were primarily responsible for reviving south-east Asian regionalism in 1966–7. Of greatest importance was the fall from power of Indonesian President Sukarno, who had been pursuing a policy of 'confrontation' against Malaysia which had raised tension throughout the region. The more pragmatic regime of President Suharto, which took over from Sukarno in 1967, was quick to express an interest in reconciliation with Malaysia, while similar moves were made to heal the Malaysia–Philippines rift. Secondly, all of south-east Asia felt threatened by the increasingly ferocious war in Vietnam. Thailand saw that it could be the next 'domino' to fall should the Communists achieve victory in South Vietnam, while the military might of North Vietnam clearly undermined the security of all south-east Asian nations. This was particularly so in view of the signals of an eventual American military withdrawal that had begun to appear at about this time. Thirdly, China was going through a period of left-wing extremism in the Cultural Revolution which had international repercussions in the form of calls to Asian Communist parties to embark upon 'peoples' wars'. China, both as a major power and as the origin of the influential minority groups of 'overseas Chinese' had always been regarded with suspicion in south-east Asia, and this radical phase made it a source of regional instability as well. Finally, there were strong economic arguments in favour of closer association, including the need for a collective response to the rise of Japanese economic power.

The Foreign Ministers of Indonesia, Malaysia, the Philippines, Singapore and Thailand established ASEAN by a Declaration in Bangkok on 8 August 1967. There is a deliberate vagueness about some of its provisions which was intended to keep the Association as flexible and open-ended as possible. There was, for example, a hint that ASEAN might be concerned with regional security in the statement that the signatories 'are determined to ensure their stability and security from external interference in any form or manifestation', and in the following assertion that 'all foreign bases are temporary and remain only with the expressed concurrence of the countries concerned'. But the Declaration limits itself to the economic, social, cultural, technical, scientific and administrative fields in specifying areas where there was to be 'active collaboration and mutual assistance'. Even here no precise form of co-operation (such as progressive tariff cuts) was named. This low-key approach to the organisation was most apparent in the decision not to create an international secretariat for ASEAN but merely to have a national secretariat in each country to administer the Association's affairs.

The ASEAN Declaration reflected the lack of any substantial common interests amongst its members beyond their apprehensions about their future security. South-east Asia is divided ethnically and in cultural/religious terms, with Christians, Muslims and Buddhists dominant in different countries. Even on security matters the ASEAN states did not have identical perceptions of the threat facing them or the best strategy for dealing with it.[56]

For these reasons ASEAN remained for the first few years little more than an affirmation of good intentions on the part of its five members. As one observer puts it: 'ASEAN in concert has been distinguished by resolutions rather than resolve, with some more pious than others.' None the less, some slow progress was made towards defining common goals and, more importantly in some respects, the rest of the world became accustomed to regarding the five as, in some senses, an entity. In November 1971 the ASEAN states issued a joint statement declaring their desire to see south-east Asia recognised as a 'Zone of Peace, Freedom and Neutrality, free from any form or manner of interference by outside powers'.[57] But the impact of this was lessened by the evident determination of Thailand and the Philippines to retain their close links with the United States. On major foreign policy questions which did not touch directly upon the ASEAN region itself, there was some co-ordination of policy — for instance over the Middle East. A significant breakthrough came with President Nixon's visit to China in 1972 and the considerable thaw which ensued in China's relations with the rest of the world. This removed at one stroke a major pillar of the structure of alignments and enmities which had prevailed in Asia for twenty years, and ASEAN, with some reluctance on Indonesia's part, was able to agree at a 1972 ministerial meeting to begin the process of improving relations with China.[58]

However, ASEAN remained primarily a consultative arrangement amongst its members. One area in particular where progress had been disappointing was that of economic relations, with intraregional trade actually having declined from 18·3 per cent of total trade in 1966 to 12·8 per cent in 1974.[59] In 1973 a UN report, 'Economic Cooperation for ASEAN', had urged the group to work towards the creation of a free trade area by 1990,[60] and a growing chorus of local business interests could be heard singing the praises of economic integration. Other countries and groups also found it convenient to deal with ASEAN as a bloc — the five had been building up a joint relationship with the European Community since 1972. But the greatest spur to increasing co-operation came in 1975 with the Communist takeover of

South Vietnam and Cambodia in the wake of the American withdrawal from Indo-China. This prompted ASEAN's leaders to embark upon a round of bilateral meetings in 1975, including one in July between the Filipino President and the Thai Prime Minister, who issued a joint communiqué calling for progress towards the regional harmonisation of industrial and agricultural policies and steps towards economic integration, including the establishment of a free trade area 'as an initial measure'.[61]

The culmination of this round of bilateral diplomacy came with the first ASEAN summit conference at Bali in April 1976. This two-day meeting produced a Treaty of Amity and Co-operation in South-east Asia in which ASEAN members pledged themselves to seek a peaceful settlement of their disputes with each other by referring them to a High Council of Ministers for mediation, inquiry or conciliation. The five leaders also confirmed earlier decisions by their Foreign Ministers to set up a central secretariat at Jakarta, to replace the separate national secretariats, and to increase from four to eleven the number of ASEAN's specialised committees. On the economic front the leaders agreed to embark upon five major industrial projects which were to serve the region as a whole, and declared their longer-term intention to proceed towards a preferential trading system.

The Bali summit also broached the controversial question of security co-operation which had been mooted from time to time in the past but without any consensus view being formed. The subject had always aroused the suspicion and hostility of the Communist powers in the region. In a 'Declaration of ASEAN Concord' the leaders confined themselves to a statement that members would continue their security co-operation on a bilateral, rather than an ASEAN basis, and in an attempt to reassure the Communist government of a now unified Vietnam they insisted that they saw their security primarily in terms of their own internal development rather than opposition to any external power. As President Suharto put it: 'Our concept of security is inward-looking, namely to establish an orderly, peaceful and stable condition within each individual territory, free from any subversive elements and infiltration wherever their origins might be.'[62] Indeed the very fact that the most serious security problems faced by the ASEAN nations stemmed from internal insurrection was a major consideration weighing against any prospect of ASEAN turning itself into a formal alliance: such a move could be a pointless provocation of Vietnam. But the number and scope of consultations amongst ASEAN members over security questions continued to grow throughout the 1970s. Thailand and Indonesia held joint naval exercises, while there were bilateral agreements over border security between Thailand and Malaysia, Malaysia and Singapore and Malaysia and Indonesia. Moreover military spending by the ASEAN nations increased sharply, with the 1980 combined total reaching £2·75 billion, an increase of 45 per cent over the previous year.[63] In addition, Singapore was building itself up as a centre for manufacturing the region's weaponry, in line with moves towards standardisation of weapons throughout ASEAN. Significantly, it was reported in 1981 that the pattern of arms purchases had shifted away from weapons for counter-insurgency towards conventional weaponry that would be used against an external aggressor.[64] All these developments led some observers to the conclusion that ASEAN was indeed becoming a *de facto* alliance.

Equally important advances were being made in economic co-operation, albeit rather slowly for the tastes of those, such as the Singaporean entrepreneurs, who felt that economic logic seemed to dictate further integration in order to achieve economies of scale. ASEAN began to adopt a united front in the international economic negotiations of the 1970s and important trade dialogues were initiated with the United States, Japan and the EEC. ASEAN as a whole was second only to the United States it its share of Japanese trade, and much effort went into improving ASEAN's economic relationship with Japan. Japan itself proved responsive to united pressure from ASEAN over such matters as its production of synthetic rubber, which competed with south-east Asia's natural rubber production.[65] The advantages of functioning as a bloc for economic purposes became apparent in 1977 when Japan granted one billion dollars of economic aid to assist in the development of the five industrial complementation projects that had been agreed at the Bali summit, setting as a main condition of the aid that these had to be established as joint ASEAN projects.[66] By 1980 these projects were all under way, and to their number had been added plans to link all the ASEAN states through underwater cables and to establish an emergency rice reserve for the region.[67] In 1980 a major EEC—ASEAN Co-operation Agreement was signed, in which the two sides agreed to work together over a wide range of development related areas. A further step towards economic integration came with the initiation of a preferential trading system in February 1977. By June 1981 over 6000 items had been included in a preferential tariff list for the region.

These developments still leave ASEAN some considerable distance from the level of integration achieved in Western Europe. But the process of regional co-operation in south-east Asia has now achieved a momentum that would be difficult to halt. One of the interesting features of ASEAN is that it has progressed so far without any sort of formal blueprint for integration other than the vague commitments of the ASEAN Declaration. This makes it difficult to predict what the next stages of regionalism will be. One possibility is for the widening of the community. In 1981 Sri Lanka applied to join ASEAN, while India has also expressed interest in some form of association. There has been some speculation about a possible 'Pacific Basin Community' being created, which would link ASEAN with the successful economies of east Asia and perhaps to Australia, New Zealand and the United States. The ASEAN members themselves appear to want to develop links with the Communist states of Indo-China, which they see as contributing to the reduction of tension in the region.

CONCLUSION

The assumption is commonly found in political science literature on regionalism that regional organisations should be measured against a single yardstick: the extent to which they contribute to the political and economic integration of their members. The ultimate goal is federation under one government. The distance travelled by a regional organisation towards that goal determines its success or lack of it. The practical experience of the three main institutions examined here shows that this may be a misguided approach, for none is in any sense close to substantial integration yet all have served a purpose in quite distinct ways that have little to do with any longer-term process of integration.

The OAS has provided an arena for the working out of the relationship between the United States and Latin America, in the course of which it has also played other roles in disseminating information, promoting economic development, settling disputes, devising common policies, and negotiating positions for some of the important international conferences. The OAU has had only a marginal significance in the resolution of disputes and even less in economic affairs. Far from its members growing in unity, as has been the case of ASEAN and to a lesser extent the Latin American members of the OAS, some of their conflicts have become increasingly bitter. But it has survived because it has performed other important functions. It has laid down norms and guidelines that have had a remarkable durability and measure of acceptance, notably over the maintenance of the territorial *status quo*. It has provided a means of arriving at an African consensus over issues such as colonialism and racism and has helped to internationalise these questions. It has gradually gained acceptance as a source of international legitimisation, and it has acted almost as a compass for foreign powers trying to steer a safe course through the turbulent waters of African politics.

ASEAN, too, started life in unpromising circumstances, with serious disputes amongst its members and few common interests beyond a general unease about the future of their region. It lacked a plan for gradual political and economic integration and for some years appeared to be an inactive irrelevance. But merely by bringing its members into regular contact with each other it helped to defuse their own conflicts and obliged them to seek consensus viewpoints on various matters. It encouraged a habit of consultation which grew inevitably into collaboration over matters of substance. Even more than the OAU it provided a focal point for outside powers as well as industrial corporations, while it also added to its members' capacity to deal on equal terms with the latter.

6 International Regimes

The process of international organisation is concerned with the development by states of ways of regulating their conflicts, jointly managing for their collective benefit various specific areas of activity and, most ambitiously, planning for peaceful change towards agreed goals. Frequently this involves the creation of large, multi-purpose institutions like the League or the UN, or of structures with more limited functions, like the Postal Union. However, the essential core of international organisation is not the various administrative or judicial bodies as such but the rules, regulations and agreed procedures for which the institutions assume responsibility. In this sense the main thrust of international organisation is the development of 'international regimes': sets of rules which aim to regulate some specific activity of international interest. Thus defined, regimes encompass not only formal institutions but many informal, decentralised arrangements amongst states.[1] Although international regimes have existed for many years, scholarly attention has only recently come to focus on the regimes as a separate analytical category from the institutional frameworks which sometimes accompany them. This increasing interest stems from three factors. Firstly, international regimes have proliferated in recent years. Secondly, they have enjoyed more success than some of the larger institutions, partly because they have invariably been founded upon an international consensus and to date allocated narrow, specific and modest objectives. Finally, a number of proposals for new regimes have been advanced which, if accepted, could have profound and exciting implications for future international relations.

A complete list of regimes would embrace almost every area of international life which is marked by some degree of orderliness and co-operation amongst states. Technical fields such as civil aviation, meteorology or telecommunications, a large part of international economic and monetary relations and certain aspects of arms control are amongst the subjects of contemporary regimes. The different forms taken by the regimes range from substantial formal institutions such as the World Health Organisation (WHO), which is actually the parent body of several smaller regimes,[2] to a treaty approved by the UN General Assembly in December 1979 declaring that the moon and its natural resources are the common heritage of mankind and hence not subject to national appropriation.[3] Here we shall consider four regimes which either exist already, are about to be established, or have merely been proposed, but which all involve significant and controversial issues.

THE THIRD UN CONFERENCE ON THE LAW OF THE SEA

The international law of the sea has always related to matters of vital importance to all states. Traditionally it has been most concerned with precisely defining the rights of navigation through various kinds of waters: the 'territorial sea' of coastal states, which is under their absolute sovereignty, narrow straits lying between two or more sovereign powers, and other international waterways. Some of these issues have long been in dispute, notably the exact extent of states' entitlements to territorial seas, but with increasing reliance being placed on the sea as a source of food, oil and, in the near future, minerals such as manganese, copper, nickel and cobalt, and with strategic and ecological problems also involved, potential areas of contention have accumulated in recent years. It is with these questions that the world's longest-lasting and, with 158 participants, largest international conference has been concerned: the Third UN Conference on the Law of the Sea (UNCLOS III). The Conference is important because its decisions are likely to determine the main features of the law of the sea across a very broad spectrum for many years and also because of the implications of its most unusual proposal: that an international authority to supervise mining the seabed of the high seas should be established.

The first UNCLOS was held in Geneva in 1958: it succeeded in drafting four conventions on the territorial sea, fishing and the conservation of the living resources of the high seas, the high seas themselves, and the rights of states to the exploitable resources of their continental shelves where these extended beyond states' territorial waters. The main purpose of the Conference was to clarify the limits to the power of coastal states outside their territorial waters, to which end it determined that states on the high seas had freedom of navigation and of fishing, the freedom to lay submarine cables and pipelines and the freedom to fly over the high seas.[4]

Although the 1958 UNCLOS was successful in its attempt to codify many aspects of marine law for the first time, some crucial difficulties were still unresolved. In particular, the exact extent of a state's legitimate territorial waters — a matter of growing controversy since 1945 — had yet to be determined, with claims ranging from the traditional three miles to twelve miles and beyond. A second UNCLOS in 1960 just failed to reach agreement on this question, but already many new problems were emerging and it soon became clear that a completely fresh approach to the law of the sea was needed. This was the task of UNCLOS III, which opened in Caracas in 1973 and whose final session is expected in 1982, provided the administration of the American President, Ronald Reagan, can overcome some misgivings it has expressed about agreements already reached.[5]

Although the negotiators at UNCLOS III have tended to view all the issues before them as part of a single package, this has largely been because many states have insisted that decisions should be reached through a complex process of consensus formation, which has meant that compromises over one issue could be traded off against concessions in another area, so all topics become inseparable from each other for bargaining purposes.[6] In practice, however, the outcome of the Conference will be several distinct regimes, each with different implications.

Many questions before UNCLOS III have now been effectively settled, notably as a result of a successful session in 1980, which was described by the leading American delegate, Elliott Richardson, as 'the most significant single event in the history of peaceful co-operation and development of the rule of law since the founding of the United Nations itself'.[7] Amongst the matters now broadly agreed upon is a twelve-mile territorial sea, with accepted rights of transit through one hundred international straits which, being less than twenty-four miles wide, would normally come under coastal state jurisdiction. Agreement has also been reached on environmental protection, marine research and the system to be employed in settling disputes.

One of several novel concepts to be given legitimacy by UNCLOS III was the principle that states should enjoy an exclusive zone (EEZ) of 200 miles from their coastline, giving them the sole right to the food and mineral resources of the sea and seabed in this area. All other states would have freedom of navigation and overflight in the zone as well as the freedom to lay submarine cables and pipelines. Coastal states would also have the obligation to pursue sound conservation measures in their EEZs.

The most contentious and complex issue before UNCLOS III has concerned the establishment of an international regime for the exploration and exploitation of the mineral resources of the deep seabed (that is beyond the EEZ limits). At stake is a potentially rich harvest of 'manganese nodules', polymetallic substances for which the technology now exists to engage in economic mining operations. The starting point for discussions on this matter was a General Assembly resolution in December 1970 declaring these resources to be 'the common heritage of mankind', but debate soon resolved itself into a conflict between three distinct interest groups. The developing countries at first insisted that mining should be carried out by an international authority in the interests of all. This they saw as an important and concrete application of their more general argument in favour of a new international economic order. The opening bargaining position of the richer industrialised nations was that any international authority should have only minimal powers, with the seabed open for any state to exploit: a situation which would naturally have suited them very well as they alone possess the necessary technology. A third group of 'landlocked and geographically disadvantaged' states, who potentially stood to be the biggest losers, have attempted to ensure that their interests have been safeguarded in any projected new regime. An additional, much smaller interest group has been the existing producers of the minerals involved, whose concern has been to place a production ceiling on seabed mining with the aim of preventing prices from falling because of overproduction.[8]

After several years of protracted argument, with compromises made on all sides, UNCLOS III was able to reach agreement on the main features of a new seabed mining regime in 1980, although the Reagan administration is still reconsidering its predecessors' acceptance of this package. The central element in the regime is to be an International Seabed Authority able to conduct its own mining operations through an institution to be called the Enterprise, which will have overall control of all seabed mining. An ingenious rule designed to ensure that the big mining companies with their vast resources and monopoly of technology would be incapable of denying the Authority its fair share of future mining operations sets out the principle that any company wanting to mine the deep seabed will first be obliged to ask for a licence to mine in two areas. The Enterprise will then grant a licence for one of these areas only, reserving the other for its own future use. It will also receive a tax from mining carried out by private or state companies.[9]

Another novel aspect of the Authority is its decision-making processes, which were at first a source of profound disagreement. In 1980 provisional agreement was reached on establishing two decision-making bodies, a Council and an Assembly, with a complex system for arriving at decisions designed to encourage consensus formation so that all interests may be safeguarded. Decisions will be divided into three categories of importance, requiring three different degrees of consensus.[10]

Other issues which are yet to be decided include the means by which the Enterprise will obtain the initial funding for its first mining operations (that is before it becomes self-financing), the rate of taxation to be imposed on mining companies, and the levels of production ceilings and the means by which and proportions into which the Authority's revenues will be shared. There has also been much debate on the important question of how mining technology, which is at present in the hands of a few countries, will be made available both to the Authority and to the less-developed countries.

If, as seems probable, the Seabed Authority is established on the basis of the 1980 agreements, it will have a growing significance in the coming decades. It represents one of the best practical opportunities for implementing the Third World's demands for a more just international economic order, especially since it would not involve a redistribution of wealth from rich to poor since it concerns resources which the rich countries do not actually possess. Its importance in the history of international organisation is also considerable. UNCLOS III itself was a landmark in the development of the consensus method of international negotiations and will doubtless serve as a model in future exercises in multilateral diplomacy. Much the same can be said of the Authority, as its decisions will also be based on consensus formation. However, the chief significance of the Authority may well reside in the fact that it will be the first international institution with a source of finance independent of governments — and potentially substantial finance because it will both mine in its own right and levy a tax on all other mining operations.

HUMAN RIGHTS

Traditionally international law is concerned solely with the rights and duties of states in their relations with each other. The sovereignty of states — the guiding doctrine of contemporary international society — has in particular precluded the international community from any responsibility for the rights of individuals or from any role with regard to a state's treatment of its own citizens. In a formal sense individuals were only accorded a personality in international law by virtue of their membership of a state. The UN's Article 2.7 enshrines the principle that states alone are responsible for matters falling within their domestic jurisdiction.

There have always been some exceptions to the general rule of no international involvement in human rights questions. Last century the practice of slavery was outlawed as a result of international pressure. Similarly, there were European interventions against Turkish mistreatment of Christian subjects of the Ottoman empire. Some would even argue that 'humanitarian interventions' are in fact permitted under international law.[11] But only since 1945 have much more extensive claims been advanced for the right of the international community to concern itself with the protection of human rights. This changed attitude was prompted most immediately by the atrocities committed by the fascist powers before and during the Second World War. Early evidence of a new international approach to human rights came with the UN Charter, which contained seven references to human rights.[12] Since then several developments have contributed to the emergence of a multi-faceted international human rights regime, comprising both global and regional arrangements and ranging in authority from documents with little more than declaratory significance to substantial and influential institutions.

The most universal, but probably least effective part of the human rights regime is that deriving from the activities of the various bodies of the UN. The central UN body here is the Human Rights Commission, which operates under the auspices of the Economic and Social Council. Its first task was to draw up a Universal Declaration of Human Rights, which was passed by the General Assembly on 10 December 1948 with South Africa, Saudi Arabia and the Soviet bloc abstaining. This represents the first attempt to arrive at an agreed international definition of human rights, and contains thirty articles which are mainly concerned with setting out traditional civil and political rights such as equality before the law, freedom from arbitrary arrest and freedom of peaceful assembly. Article 28 is interesting in that it states the right of all to 'a social and international order in which the rights and freedoms set out in this Declaration can be fully realised'. This clearly articulates the principle that individual rights within states are to some extent dependent upon the nature of the system of relations between states. Apart from the Declaration the Commission has also been responsible for drawing up several conventions on special aspects of human rights, such as the 1966 Convention on the Elimination of All Forms of Racial Discrimination. A major task during the 1960s was drafting two Covenants, which were intended to have greater legal force. One of these covers civil and political rights, while the other is concerned with economic, social and cultural rights, the separate treatment of these two areas reflecting a divergence of opinion as to which was the more important. The Covenants were agreed in December 1966, but did not achieve the necessary number of ratifications to acquire legal status until 1973.[13]

The UN has at its disposal only insubstantial means of implementing and enforcing its various pronouncements on human rights. It organises seminars and conferences on a wide variety of human rights issues, with forty-two such meetings taking place between 1957 and 1973.[14] The Commission publishes a *Human Rights Yearbook* which, however, contains primarily information supplied by governments. In March 1974 a special sub-Commission was established to look into 'situations which reveal a consistent pattern of gross violations of human rights' as a means of bringing stronger pressure to bear on particular governments[15] (who, unfortunately, if genuinely guilty would presumably be those least likely to take any notice of moral injunctions from the UN).

A new Human Rights Committee, established in 1977 under Article 28 of the Covenant for Civil and Political Rights, can evaluate the record of states in implementing the Covenant and receive petitions from individuals whose states have ratified the Optional Protocol to the Covenant. In specific instances the UN has set up its own fact-finding groups so that it does not need to rely solely on evidence provided by governments. But here it has been thwarted by the refusal of the governments concerned to co-operate — for example in the case of a group appointed to investigate human rights in territories occupied by Israel in 1967.[16]

In the present state of world politics many of the obstacles to a universal system for the protection of human rights seem insuperable. At the most basic level there are profound differences of opinion as to how human rights should be defined and which category of rights should have priority in international deliberations. Even such a central principle as the right to life is defined differently in various UN and regional documents in line with different points of view on capital punishment and abortion. However, the greatest divergence occurs between those who emphasise the traditional civil and political rights and those who would rather give priority to economic and social rights. The problem is partly ideological: the traditional rights tend to concentrate upon the limits to the power of the state *vis-à-vis* individuals, a concern that runs counter to the values and interests of those societies where the state's requirements are seen as supreme, as in the Soviet bloc, where economic rights, such as the right to work, are given priority. There is also an argument advanced by many Third World countries that to stress the freedom of the individual and such rights as a free press and free elections is meaningless and may be counterproductive in societies where even the most basic standards of material well-being and literacy are yet to be attained.[17] This view is enshrined in the Covenant on Economic, Social and Cultural Rights, whose preamble states that 'the ideal of free human beings enjoying freedom from fear and want can only be achieved if conditions are created whereby everyone may enjoy his economic, social and cultural rights as well as his civil and political rights'. Third World countries also frequently stress collective rather than individual rights, such as the right of national self-determination or the right of racial equality.

Perhaps the greatest barrier to a universal human rights regime is the fact that in a world with many fierce interstate antagonisms, moves towards a system for the international protection of human rights will inevitably be exploited for diplomatic or propaganda purposes by one state against another. Such favourite targets of the Third World as South Africa and Israel have felt the full force, such as it is, of the UN's human rights machinery, while equally bad (or far worse) offenders like Idi Amin's Uganda have escaped relatively lightly.[18] In the early years of the UN, the then American-dominated General Assembly tended to focus its attention mainly on human rights violations in the Soviet bloc, and Soviet spokesmen have claimed that the concern shown by Washington in the 1970s for human rights in the world had a similar anti-Soviet purpose.[19]

Finally, even if international relations were marked more than they are by good will and ideological consensus, the doctrine of state sovereignty would still prevent the development of an effective rights regime. South Africa, Israel, the Soviet Union and others accused in the UN of human rights violations have all responded by asserting their right to govern their internal affairs as they choose. Indeed, there is much force to their argument. While states are sovereign in their responsibilities, in that they alone accept ultimate liability for their security or economic welfare, they will see little reason to relinquish their sovereign rights and powers. Hence, progress towards an effective universal human rights regime is dependent upon more fundamental changes in the nature of international relations from a sovereignty-based pluralist system to the as yet unrealistic ideal of a world community.

This factor partly explains the relative success of some regionally based human rights regimes, since they developed amongst states which already enjoy considerable economic and military integration. The work of many regional organisations often has implications for human rights, but only the American and Western European regions have extensive systems for the promotion and protection of human rights. The American system is based, in principle, upon the 1948 American Declaration on the Rights and Duties of Man.[20] This was followed by the formation of an Inter-American Commission on Human Rights in 1959, whose powers were broadened in 1965 following several successful initiatives by the Commission, notably in promoting the rights of political prisoners and refugees in the Dominican Republic.[21] In 1969 an American Convention on human rights was drawn up, which by 1978 had come into effect amongst eleven ratifying states (not including the United States).[22]

Given the notoriety of many Latin American countries in the human rights field, the American human rights system can hardly be acclaimed as a great success. Indeed, it should perhaps be remembered that no unrealistic expectations were held of the Commission from the outset, merely that it should promote an awareness of and respect for human rights in the region. It was given no powers to force states to adhere to the Declaration, nor were any sanctions envisaged. Within these limitations it has performed its task with some success. It has gradually become bolder in its interpretation of its role, and has moved from its original function of preparing studies and reports to direct criticisms of individual states. But in all Latin American affairs much hangs on the attitude taken by the United States. One early justification for persecution in the region was that it was necessary to combat Communism, in line with Washington's cold war preoccupations.[23] In the 1970s, when Congress and President Carter decided to make American aid dependent on recipient countries' human rights record, the worst Latin American cases came under considerable pressure. Now President Reagan has begun to reverse this emphasis. With such fluidity in American policy, even the violators of human rights in Latin America might be forgiven for some uncertainty as to how to conduct themselves to gain US support.

By contrast with Latin America, in Western Europe the regional human rights machinery has had a significant and growing impact. This was partly because the impetus given to the movement towards the international protection of human rights by the Second World War was naturally greatest in the region where the greatest violations had taken place, and partly because, for the first time in European history, all Western European nations found themselves with democratic governments devoted to the principle of the rule of law.

The parent body of the European human rights system is the Council of Europe, set up in 1949 and consisting of eighteen members, including Turkey, Malta, Switzerland and Sweden. The Council drew up a European Convention of Human Rights, which came into force in 1953. Three separate organs administer the system for implementing the protection of the rights agreed in the Convention. The European Commission for Human Rights receives petitions from both states and (the overwhelming majority of cases) individuals. Its first task is to determine whether petitions are admissible for further consideration, with several grounds existing for rejecting a petition, including that 'local remedies' have not been exhausted and the rather sweeping powers of Article 27 (2) to reject any petition that is 'manifestly ill-founded'.[24] Most petitions fail at this first hurdle, and in the case of those deemed admissible, the Commission's first task is to seek to obtain a 'friendly settlement'. For instance, in several cases the offending state has amended a relevant law before a petition could progress further through the European system, thus enbling the Commission to drop the matter. At this stage the Commission is also empowered to undertake a fact-finding investigation, with member states required to provide it with all necessary facilities for this purpose. The Commission may then express its opinion on a petition and pass this on for consideration by a Committee or Minister or, normally where some complex point of law is involved, it may request a third body, the European Human Rights Court, to reach a judgement. All the Commission's decisions are arrived at by majority vote.

Democratic states with a free press are inevitably sensitive to accusations that they have violated human rights and the mere fact of a petition proceeding as far as the Court has often served to give an issue sufficient publicity to bring about a change in law or practice. The Court also has more direct powers, including its capacity under Article 50 to 'afford just satisfaction to the injured party'. The ultimate sanction is for a state to be expelled from the Council of Europe, as might have happened to Greece when it was under military government, had Greece not forestalled this by withdrawing from the Council.

The European human rights system has had an extraordinary success in redressing individual wrongs, causing the law of several countries to be amended, helping to bring the different legal systems of Western Europe into some harmony with each other, and generally increasing awareness of the many issues involved in human rights questions. Moreover, its influence and prestige seem to be growing. Several explanations have been offered for this success, including the confidence of member states that the screening system will let through only a small minority of complaints, that proceedings will be private and that states will not abuse the system to score points off each other. But of central importance is the fact that the system operates among states where there are already, for the most part, effective domestic safeguards of human rights. The Convention itself merely enshrines rights which have existed in law for many years in several member countries, and the primary role of the European system has been to identify marginal areas where the domestic legal processes contain loopholes or have been bypassed. This raises questions about the European system's value as a model for the international protection of human rights elsewhere, and about its effectiveness in cases where states do not already have a high regard for human rights, as evidenced by the withdrawal of Greece's military regime. As is so often the case in the history of international organisation, changes in the attitudes of states are the crucial element which must precede the creation of effective international instruments. But once such changes have occurred, institutions like the European system may play an important part in safeguarding existing rights and lay the foundations for further progress.

INTERNATIONAL TERRORISM

Calls for a regime to deal with international terrorism have been heard with increasing frequency since this phenomenon first came into prominence in the late 1960s. Numerous attempts have been made at both regional and global levels to reach agreement on international co-operation to meet the problems, but these have generally met with little success for reasons which also illustrate the more general problems of developing international law in politically highly charged areas.

There are fundamental difficulties in defining 'terrorism' and indeed 'international' in this context.[25] Aerial hijackings, kidnappings of foreign diplomats and businessmen, bombing outrages: all are associated in the popular mind with the term 'international terrorism'. But when it comes to defining the common elements in all such activities in clear legal terminology that is acceptable to governments of several ideological persuasions as the basis of an international code of conduct, difficulties soon appear. The most obvious difficulty is that an act of violence which may be thought reprehensible in one context can seem morally acceptable in another, and the dividing line between the two is seldom clear-cut or identical for all observers. Few Arab nations would agree to include acts of violence committed in the name of Palestinian liberation within a system of international constraints against terrorism; African states would likewise exclude liberation movements in South Africa or Namibia, while many in the West would have similar reservations about political offences committed in Eastern Europe. Beyond this there is the larger moral and philosophical question of the validity of the state's claim to the sole legitimate use of violence, a claim which is the ultimate source of the distinction between violence carried out by soldiers and other agents of the state and similar acts committed for political ends by unofficial groups.

Even if governments did not have their own political reasons for their caution in accepting all-embracing rules relating to international terrorism, there would still be many problems. The offences that are usually brought together under the label of 'international terrorism' are, on closer examination, different in their nature and, in practical terms, require different responses. Even that quality which makes the offences 'international' is not beyond dispute. Does the target of the terrorist have to be foreign or is terrorism international simply when there is an underlying aim of promoting world revolution? What about terrorist acts committed inside a country by nationals of that country who have close links with a global terrorist network? Does the term include terrorism by foreigners on behalf of one side in an internal conflict in, for example, Israel or South Africa? Is the phenomenon the same whether governments or private agencies are responsible?

Early attempts were made in the League of Nations to develop an anti-terrorist regime, but little of consequence happened in this area until the 1960s. An increasing number of aircraft hijackings prompted a series of international conventions designed to deal with the problems, beginning with the 1963 Tokyo Convention on Offences and Certain Other Acts Committed on Board Aircraft, which came into force in 1969. This was primarily concerned with establishing the principles governing the responsibility for safe return of the aircraft.[26]

The Convention did not contain provisions for the mandatory extradition of hijackers, punishment being left to the domestic laws of the state which apprehended them. An attempt was made to bridge these gaps in two later conventions, the 1970 Hague Convention for the Suppression of the Unlawful Seizure of Aircraft and the 1971 Montreal Convention for the Suppression of Unlawful Acts Against the Safety of Civil Aviation. The first of these set out the principle that states should either extradite a hijacker or prosecute him according to their own domestic laws, but it also accepted the longstanding exception in international law to extradition where political offences were involved. The Montreal Convention was aimed at widening the range of offences under international law relating to aircraft to include, for instance, violence against airports or grounded aircraft.

Although the Montreal Convention in particular broke new ground in international law, it left untouched two basic problems — quite apart from the fact that it only applied to those states which ratified it.[27] The first was that it excepted political offenders from extradition requirements, following a time-honoured tradition of political asylum. This gave an escape clause to states which for various reasons were reluctant to hand over or even prosecute themselves certain categories of terrorist. Such international co-operation as there has been over comprehensive extradition procedures has taken place at a bilateral or regional level. Perhaps the most important move here was the adoption in November 1976 by the Council of Europe of a Convention on the Suppression of Terrorism whose aim, stated in Article One, was to ensure that a specified range of acts could not be excused on the grounds that they were politically motivated. Such offences included anything within the scope of the Hague and Montreal Conventions as well as serious offences against internationally protected persons, such as diplomats, and any offence involving kidnapping or the taking of hostages.[28] However, so far as the larger international community is concerned, there are still serious barriers against the adoption of such a clause. For instance, in December 1979 the UN General Assembly passed a Convention against the taking of hostages, but one article listed extensive exceptions to extradition requirements, namely where there were substantial grounds for believing that the offender might be punished 'on account of his race, religion, nationality, ethnic origin or political opinion'.

The second problem with the Hague and Montreal Conventions was that they contained no provision for sanctions to be imposed against states which violated them by, for example, harbouring terrorists. A conference of the International Civil Aviation Organisation (ICAO) debated the question of a separate convention which would impose sanctions on delinquent states, but failed because a sizeable section of delegates insisted that priority should be given to tackling the issues which, in their view, prompted political hijackings, notably, of course, the Palestinian question.[29] More limited initiatives have had greater success. In 1978 a joint declaration by the United States, Canada, West Germany, Japan, France, Britain and Italy stated that a boycott on air traffic would be imposed against countries refusing either to extradite or prosecute hijackers and return captured aircraft.[30] Perhaps the most significant form of pressure has come from airline pilots themselves, who have naturally felt aggrieved at the failure of governments to agree to firm measures against hijacking. In 1968 a threat by the airline pilots association to boycott all flights to Algeria brought the speedy release of the crew and passengers on an Israeli plane that had been hijacked there.[31] Similar threats of strike action have prodded governments into discussing sanctions against states who harbour hijackers.

Diplomats have been another prime target of international terrorism. International law has long maintained that states receiving diplomats have a fundamental duty to protect them and these ancient principles are enshrined in more recent documents, such as the Vienna Convention on Diplomatic Relations. However, an escalation in kidnappings and other acts of violence against diplomats since 1960 revealed inadequacies in the traditional international law relating to diplomats. As with hijacking, there have been problems in extraditing offenders from certain states which are prepared to harbour them, and the Convention does not lay down any agreed procedures for preventing and punishing acts of terrorism against diplomats. More recent international agreements have tried to go a stage further than the Vienna Convention but with only limited success. These include a 1971 OAS Convention which has won little support, despite the frequency of terrorist incidents involving diplomats in South America, and a 1973 UN General Assembly Convention which, however, does not oblige states to prosecute persons committing crimes against diplomats in all circumstances without exception.

It is clear that an anti-terrorist regime exists, at best, only in an embryonic and diffuse form. This is partly for the reasons suggested earlier and partly because, despite its headline-grabbing capacity, international terrorism is not yet seen as inflicting unacceptable damage upon states. However, it is worth noting that this is a case of a regime where informal co-operation and tacit agreements amongst states may carry more weight than formal conventions and public agreements. Israel's 1976 Entebbe raid to release 108 Israeli hostages held in Uganda by Palestinians who had hijacked a plane there, and similarly decisive action in 1977 by West Germany to release hostages held at Mogadishu airport, Somalia, and by Britain in 1980 to free hostages from the Iranian embassy in London, were certainly of great significance in demonstrating the resolve of at least some governments to deal firmly with international terrorism.

THE NEW INTERNATIONAL ECONOMIC ORDER[32]

By far the most ambitious proposals for a new international regime are to be found in the demands in recent years from many Third World countries for the creation of a new international economic order (NIEO). This demand was first made explicit at the Sixth Special Session of the UN General Assembly in April 1974, although claims by developing countries for more equitable treatment in the world economy had been heard since 1945.[33] Notable landmarks since then included the first Afro-Asian Conference at Bandung in 1955, which called for raw materials prices to be stabilised and for Third World countries to have a larger share in the processing of raw materials, where the greatest profits were to be obtained.[34] The 1960s were declared the first UN 'Development Decade', while in 1964 the first UN Conference on Trade and Development (UNCTAD) was held in Geneva. This was institutionalised and given its own Secretariat, so it soon became the main forum for Third World countries on international economic matters. The Third World states united into a block for negotiating purposes, naming themselves the Group of 77 after the original number of developing countries attending. But although under-development in the Third World has been an issue in international politics for some years, the two 1974 General Assembly resolutions on an NIEO reflected a significant shift in Third World opinion away from calls for marginal changes and piecemeal reforms to an insistence upon a fundamental restructuring of the international economy in favour of the developing countries. The shift was marked not just by more radical proposals but by a new mood of confrontation in the Third World, directed in the main against the Western industrialised nations. Before considering the reasons for this new atmosphere and the implications and problems of the NIEO demand, it is worth outlining the proposals upon which it is based.

The general objective of the new order, as stated in the 1974 Declaration on the Establishment of a New International Economic Order is that it should be: 'based on equity, sovereign equality, inter-dependence, common interest and co-operation among all states, irrespective of their economic and social systems [and should] correct inequalities and redress existing injustices'.[35] According to the Declaration, the NIEO should be founded on respect for twenty principles, including equal participation in the solving of world economic problems, full sovereignty of every state over its natural resources and all economic activities, supervision of the activities of transnational corporations, improvement in the terms of trade between industrialised and developing countries, reform of the international monetary system, the promotion of the transfer of technology to the Third World, and the facilitation of the role of producers' associations. Alongside the Declaration was a Programme of Action, which spelt out specific measures designed to achieve the NIEO. These included various steps to sustain commodity prices; expansion of industrialised countries' imports of products from developed countries by means of 'appropriate adjustments' in the economies of the industrialised countries; measures to maintain the real value of the currency reserves of the developing nations; Third World participation in the International Monetary Fund (IMF); the creation of additional borrowing facilities for the Third World; renegotiation of the Third World's debt burden; formulation of an international code of conduct for the transfer of technology; emulation of the actions of the Organisation of Petroleum Exporting Countries in forcing up the price of oil; and special programmes for the most needy developing nations. The 1974 UN meeting was followed by other conferences which in some respects were even more radical in their proposals. Several Third World statements asserted the right of developing countries to nationalise foreign-owned enterprises without paying the compensation required by current international law. A conference in Senegal held in February 1975 and attended by 110 developing nations blamed 'imperialism and neocolonialism' for Third World underdevelopment.[36] In March 1975 the 'Lima Declaration', issued after a conference of the UN Industrial Development Organisation (UNIDO), insisted that the developing countries' share in total world industrial production should be increased from 7 per cent to at least 25 per cent by means of a restructuring of industry in the developed countries, a reduction of trade barriers against Third World products, a change in the present system for the legal protection of patents and other measures. Meanwhile UNCTAD issued its most significant proposal, for an integrated commodity programme to maintain the prices of raw materials.[37]

A range of long- and short-term factors contributed to the emergence of the NIEO proposal in 1974. Most fundamental was the developing crisis in the existing international economic regime, which had been set up at the 1944 Bretton Woods Conference and elsewhere. This had rested on several pillars, including an American willingness and capacity to underwrite the system, and acquiescence in American leadership by other Western nations, a concentration of power in the Western world, and a broad ideological consensus that the system should be based on liberal/capitalist principles emphasising minimal government interference in the workings of the market and, in particular, the maximum possible free trade.[38] By the 1970s American strength had suffered a relative decline, rifts had appeared in the Western alliance, and a growing chorus could be heard questioning the orthodoxy of minimal intervention in the management of the international economy. Most notably, the underlying assumption of liberal economic doctrines, that a free-market system was the best way of ensuring the most efficient and equitable allocation of resources, was under increasing attack in the Third World. There an opposing radical critique had emerged in which the prevailing international economic system was seen as essentially exploitative of Third World primary producers. One of the early exponents of this view was Raul Prebisch, who became the first Secretary-General of UNCTAD. Even those moderate Third World leaders who did not share this interpretation were beginning to feel a sense of disillusionment at the failure of Western aid programmes to achieve significant results, and all were agreed upon the necessity for greater Third World participation in the major decision-making processes in the international economy.

The immediate catalyst for the more radical Third World approach was the success of the OPEC countries in forcing through a massive increase in the price of oil in 1973. This seemed at the time to many Third World primary producers to show the way for them to achieve similar gains by forming cartels to push up the prices of other commodity exports. A 'trade union' attitude quickly made itself apparent in the Third World, whereby the developing countries saw themselves as engaging in collective action *vis-à-vis* the industrialised countries to improve both their immediate export earnings and their overall bargaining position in relation to a wide range of other proposed changes in the international economic regime. Producers' associations for bauxite, tin, copper, bananas, iron ore, natural rubber, mercury, tungsten, tropical timber, manganese and pepper all tried to emulate OPEC.[39] At the same time attention came to focus upon the role played by the Western-owned transnational corporations, which had a major share in the marketing of many commodities.[40] In 1973 the UN published a report on the operations of transnational corporations in developing countries, which had a significant impact in the Third World and led to calls for a code of conduct to govern the activities of the transnational corporations.[41]

The initial response of the industrialised world seemed to contain a certain element of panic. The United States in particular attempted to counter what it viewed as a potentially serious threat of inflationary and destabilising Third World action by organising a united response amongst its allies, but this failed because of disagreements within the Western camp as to the correct policy to adopt towards OPEC and its imitators. Some European states, notably Sweden and the Netherlands, clearly believed the Third World to have a strong case. Others, such as

France, felt that basic national interests dictated a more conciliatory response than that advocated by the United States. These considerations influenced the European Community in its decision to grant a number of its former colonies a special trade and aid relationship under the terms of the Lomé Convention of 1975. In the Convention, the Community and forty-six developing countries from the African, Caribbean and Pacific region (ACP) agreed to a wide range of measures of economic co-operation; which were hailed at the time as a first step towards and possible model for a more widely based NIEO. These included free access to the Community market for 99·5 per cent of ACP exports on a non-reciprocal basis, an innovating scheme for the stabilisation of certain export earnings for the ACP (known as the Stabex system), co-ordination of existing Community aid programmes, a commitment to transfer technology to the ACP countries and joint institutions to administer the Convention. The Convention was re-negotiated in 1979 in more difficult worldwide economic circumstances and the Third World participants were generally disappointed with the results. None the less some advances were made, including improvement of access to the EEC market for some products, a widening of the Stabex schemes and the introduction of a system designed to deal with certain problems arising out of the export of a limited number of minerals. As well as participating in the Lomé Convention, France also initiated the so-called 'North–South' dialogue between a larger number of industrialised and developing countries, which took place in Paris between 1975 and 1977, but with few significant results.

Outside Europe progress towards an NIEO was even slower, a fact much remarked upon at a special UN General Assembly session in 1980. There is little doubt that the Third World countries were unfortunate in timing their demand at the beginning of a major economic recession. But even if circumstances had been far less forbidding, the NIEO proposal would still have faced many serious problems. The most fundamental objection to it is, in essence, ideological. It requires not merely intervention in the workings of the international economy, but governmental restructuring of domestic economies in the interests of the Third World: a suggestion which the most important free market economy, the United States, has rejected on the grounds that such a degree of state control of private enterprise is wholly unacceptable.[42] One practical aspect of this problem is that the NIEO proposals call for the transfer of technology from rich to poor nations, but this technology is owned largely by private companies, not states, so that a transfer could only be effected through a change in the internal economic arrangements of Western countries. Moreover, there is considerable room for doubt as to whether the NIEO, as currently proposed, would indeed benefit those most in need. Several already wealthy primary producers, such as Australia or Canada, might be richly rewarded, while some poor countries without natural resources could be hardest hit, as happened in the wake of OPEC's price-raising exercises. More significantly, perhaps, the main thrust of the Third World demands is for greater national sovereignty, something which would naturally benefit states as such but not necessarily the most disadvantaged peoples living in them. Indeed, if the poorest communities in Third World countries are truly to be aided, this could imply a practical erosion of sovereignty through, for instance, interventionist policies by the World Bank and other agencies to aid the rural poor in the Third World.[43] A further difficulty lies in the rhetorical and theoretical underpinning of the NIEO demands. Leaders of the industrialised countries are unlikely to allow themselves to be put in the position of seeming to accept an interpretation of history in which they are cast as villains, responsible for Third World underdevelopment, with the NIEO an act of atonement for past sins. Finally, some aspects of the proposed NIEO would violate certain principles in contemporary international law, notably the suggestion that developing countries should be able to nationalise foreign-owned assets with only minimal compensation.

The achievement of even a limited and partial NIEO would have major implications for international organisation. It would complete the process by which the UN has come increasingly to concern itself with global welfare rather than security; it would require international management of the world economy on a scale hitherto unheard of, with correspondingly far-reaching amendments to the decision-making structure of the UN and other institutions. Indeed it would require several new institutions to be established with similar powers to the proposed seabed authority. Quite apart from the other obstacles already mentioned, this consideration alone is likely to make progress towards the NIEO slow and difficult, if not impossible in any substantial sense. However, a few marginal but not insignificant developments might be seen in the next ten years. There has, for instance, been much discussion of the need for a new global food regime, to include a system of worldwide grain reserves. Although negotiations towards this end have so far been unsuccessful, there is at least some consensus about the necessity for such a regime even if there is often sharp disagreement as to the form it should take.[44]

A potentially significant breakthrough came in September 1981 when delegations from 142 nations attending a UN conference unanimously agreed upon a package of measures to aid the thirty-one least developed countries. Under the terms of the agreement, aid donors will guarantee the thirty-one countries 0·15 per cent of their gross national product as aid. Individual aid consortia will also be formed for any of the thirty-one who request them. The implications of the package for the NIEO proposals are threefold. It proved that it is possible for the rich and poor countries to reach a consensus on specific aspects of the NIEO. It requires the richer countries to undertake a long-term commitment in the allocation of their resources. And it is a first step towards a key element in the NIEO proposals: that the wealthier nations set aside a specific proportion of their GNPs in aid, rather than simply making their aid decisions on an *ad hoc* basis from year to year. It was also notable that discussions were marked by a more moderate and conciliatory tone from many Third World countries than had been the case when the original NIEO scheme was mooted. The agreement was described by the spokesman for the Asian group at the conference as 'a milestone in international development cooperation'.[45] Whether such an optimistic assessment is justified depends on the outcome of several crucial North—South meetings over the next few years, which will attempt to lay the foundations of a more far-reaching NIEO.

Chronological Table

1899		First Hague Conference. Permanent Court of Arbitration established
1907		Second Hague Conference
1908		Publication of Léon Bourgeois's book, *La Société des Nations*
1915	June	League to Enforce Peace established in United States
1916	May	Woodrow Wilson's first public endorsement of the League of Nations idea
1918	January	Wilson's Fourteen Points speech
1919	January	Paris Peace Conference opens
	February	The League of Nations Commission produces its first version of the Covenant
	April	Final version of Covenant
1920	March	American Senate fails to ratify Peace Treaty
1921	October	Åland Islands question settled by League Council
1923	September	Italian occupation of Corfu
1925	September	Greco–Bulgarian incident
	October	Locarno Pact
1926	September	Germany admitted to League
1931	September	Japanese moves against Manchuria
	December	Lytton Commission sent to investigate Manchurian situation
1932	March	Japan establishes puppet state in Manchuria
1933	January	Hitler becomes German Chancellor
	March	Japan withdraws from League
	June	World Economic Conference
1934	September	Soviet Union joins League
1935	October	Italian invasion of Ethiopia
	November	Economic sanctions imposed against Italy
1936	July	Spanish Civil War commences
1939	December	Soviet Union expelled from League
1944	August	Dumbarton Oaks Conference

139

1945	February	Yalta Conference
	April	United Nations Conference on International Organisation commences
	October	UN Charter comes into force
1946	January	First Security Council meeting
1947		Marshall Plan
	November	General Assembly adopts plan for partition of Palestine
1948	April	OEEC established
	May	OAS Charter agreed
	December	Universal Declaration of Human Rights
1949	May	Council of Europe formed
1950	May	Schuman Plan for Coal and Steel Community
	June	North Korea attacks South Korea
	July	UN operations in Korea commence. European Payments Union established
	October	Pléven Plan for a European Defence Community
	November	Uniting for Peace Resolution
1951	April	European Coal and Steel Community set up
	October	Organisation of Central American States formed
1952		European Defence Community fails to be adopted by French Assembly
1955	June	Messina Conference decides to move towards creation of EEC
1956	November	Establishment of United Nations Emergency Force in Middle East
1957	March	Treaty of Rome inaugurates EEC
1958		Geneva Conference on the Law of the Sea
1959		Inter-American Commission on Human Rights established
	February	Latin American Free Trade Association set up
	November	Formation of European Free Trade Association
1960	July	UN intervention in the Congo begins
1961		Alliance for Progress launched in Latin America
	February	Assassination of Patrice Lumumba in the Congo
	July	Britain applies to join EEC
	September	Death of Dag Hammarskjöld
1963	January	De Gaulle vetoes British entry into EEC
	May	OAU Charter drawn up

1964		First UNCTAD held in Geneva
	June	Withdrawal of UN force in the Congo
1965	April	Merger of executives of the three European Communities
	July	French boycott of EEC begins
	November	Ian Smith's Unilateral Declaration of Independence in Rhodesia
1966	January	Luxemburg 'gentlemen's agreement' ends EEC crisis
	December	UN adopts mandatory economic sanctions against Rhodesia
1967		Nigerian Civil War begins
	May	Second British application to join European Community
	June	Middle East War
	August	ASEAN formed
1969	April	De Gaulle resigns
	May	Andean Group formed
	December	Hague summit meeting decides to start negotiations on enlargement of EEC
1973		Third UN Conference on Law of the Sea opens
	January	Britain, Ireland and Denmark join European Community
	February	Lomé Convention signed
1974		UN General Assembly calls for new international economic order
1975	May	Economic Community of West African States established
	June	British referendum on EEC membership
	December	UN General Assembly adopts 'Zionism is racialism' resolution
1976	April	First ASEAN summit conference
1979	June	First direct elections to European Parliament
	December	Ian Smith agrees to majority rule for Rhodesia
1981	January	Greece admitted to European Community
	October	North–South Conference at Cancun

Select Bibliography

This is not a comprehensive bibliography: various primary sources and other less accessible items are fully acknowledged in the notes.

LEAGUE OF NATIONS

J. BARROS, *Betrayal from Within: Joseph Avenol, Secretary-General of the League of Nations, 1933–1940* (New York, 1969).

J. BARROS, *Office without Power: Secretary-General Sir Eric Drummond, 1919–1933* (Oxford, 1979).

M. BURTON, *The Assembly of the League of Nations* (New York, 1974).

B. DEXTER, *The Years of Opportunity: The League of Nations, 1920–1926* (New York, 1967).

G. W. EGERTON, *Great Britain and the League of Nations* (London, 1979).

A. J. MAYER, *Politics and Diplomacy of Peacemaking* (London, 1968).

D. H. MILLER, *The Drafting of the Covenant*, 2 vols (New York, 1928).

C. SEYMOUR, *The Intimate Papers of Colonel House* (London, 1928).

C. THORNE, *The Limits of Foreign Policy: The West, the League and the Far Eastern Crisis of 1931–1933* (London, 1972).

F. P. WALTERS, *A History of the League of Nations* (London, 1952).

A. ZIMMERN, *The League of Nations and the Rule of Law* (London, 1936).

UNITED NATIONS

T. M. CAMPBELL, *Masquerade Peace: America's UN Policy, 1944–45* (Tallahassee, 1973).

M. EL-AYOUTY, *The United Nations and Decolonisation* (The Hague, 1971).

L. M. GOODRICH and E. HAMBRO, *Charter of the United Nations: Commentary and Documents* (London, 1949).

G. L. GOODWIN, *Britain and the United Nations* (London, 1957).

R. HISCOCKS, *The Security Council* (London, 1973).

R. HOGGART, *An Idea and its Servants: UNESCO from Within* (London, 1978).

A. JAMES, *The Politics of Peacekeeping* (London, 1969).
D. A. KAY, *The Changing United Nations* (New York, 1977).
TRYGVE LIE, *In the Cause of Peace* (New York, 1954).
E. LUARD, *The United Nations* (London, 1979).
H. G. NICHOLAS, *The United Nations as a Political Institution* (London, 1975).
A. Z. RUBINSTEIN and G. GINSBURGS, *Soviet and American Policies in the United Nations* (New York, 1971).
J. G. STOESSINGER, *The United Nations and the Superpowers*, 3rd edn (New York, 1973).
U THANT, *View from the UN* (London, 1977).
A. VERRIER, *International Peacekeeping* (Harmondsworth, 1981).
L. D. WELLER and A. P. SIMONS, *The United States and the United Nations* (New York, 1967).
A. YESELSON and A. GAGLIONE, *A Dangerous Place* (New York, 1974).

THE EUROPEAN COMMUNITY

M. BELOFF, *The United States and the Unity of Europe* (London, 1963).
M. CAMPS, *European Unification in the Sixties* (New York, 1966).
M. HODGES (ed.), *European Integration* (London, 1972).
G. IONESCU, *The New Politics of European Integration* (London, 1972).
R. JACKSON and J. FITZMAURICE, *The European Parliament: A Guide to Direct Elections* (Harmondsworth, 1979).
R. C. MOWATT, *Creating the European Community* (London, 1973).
M. PALMER *et al.*, *European Unity: A Survey of the European Organisations* (London, 1968).
R. PRYCE, *The Politics of the European Community* (Boston, 1973).
C. SASSE *et al.*, *Decision-making in the European Community* (New York, 1977).
D. SWANN, *The Economics of the Common Market*, 4th edn (Harmondsworth, 1978).
R. VAUGHAN, *Postwar Integration in Europe* (London, 1976).
S. Z. YOUNG, *Terms of Entry: Britain's Negotiations with the European Community, 1970–1972* (London, 1973).

OTHER REGIONAL ORGANISATIONS

G. POPE ATKINS, *Latin America in the International Political System* (New York, 1977).

M. MARGARET BALL, *The OAS in Transition* (Durham: Duke University Press, 1969).

G. CONNELL-SMITH, *The Inter-American System* (London, 1966).

Y. EL-AYOUTY (ed.), *The Organisation of African Unity after Ten Years* (New York, 1976).

B. K. GORDON, *The Dimensions of Conflict in South-east Asia* (New Jersey, 1966).

A. SHLAIM (ed.), *International Organisations in World Politics, Yearbook 1975* (London, 1976).

P. A. THARP JR, *Regional International Organisations: Structures and Functions* (New York, 1971).

I. WALLERSTEIN, *Africa: The Politics of Unity* (New York, 1967).

M. WOLFERS, *Politics in the Organisation of African Unity* (London, 1976).

INTERNATIONAL REGIMES

L. ANELL and B. NYGREN, *The Developing Countries and World Economic Order* (London, 1980).

J. N. BHAGWATI (ed.), *The New International Economic Order: The North–South Debate* (Cambridge, Mass., 1977).

B. BUZAN, *Seabed Politics* (London, 1976).

J. I. DOMINGUEZ *et al.*, *Enhancing Global Human Rights* (New York, 1979).

F. DORRICK (ed.), *Human Rights* (Westmead, 1979).

G. F. ERB and V. KALLAB (eds), *Beyond Dependency* (New York, 1975).

A. E. EVANS and J. F. MURPHY, *Legal Aspects of International Terrorism* (Lexington, 1978).

F. G. JACOBS, *The European Convention on Human Rights* (Oxford, 1975).

D. KOMMERS and G. LOESHER (eds), *American Foreign Policy and Human Rights* (Belmont: Notre Dame University Press, 1979).

E. LAZLO *et al.*, *The Objectives of the New International Economic Order* (New York, 1978).

L. J. LE BLANC, *The OAS and the Promotion and Protection of Human Rights* (The Hague, 1977).

D. M. LEIVE, *International Regulatory Regimes* (Lexington: Lexington Books, 1976).

J. LODGE (ed.), *Terrorism: A Challenge to the State* (Oxford, 1981).

E. LUARD (ed.), *The International Protection of Human Rights* (London, 1967).

M. S. McDOUGAL *et al.*, *Human Rights and World Public Order* (New Haven and London, 1980).

K. P. SAUVANT and H. HASENPFLUG (eds), *The New International Economic Order* (London, 1977).

J. E. SPERO, *The Politics of International Economic Relations* (London, 1977).

P. WILKINSON, *Terrorism and the Liberal State* (London, 1977).

ARTICLES

S. BAILEY, 'UN Fact Finding and Human Rights Complaints', *International Affairs* (April 1972).

I. L. CLAUDE, 'The OAS, the UN and the United States', *International Conciliation* (March 1964).

B. V. COHEN, 'The Impact of the United Nations on United States Foreign Policy', *International Organisation* (May 1951).

G. CURRY, 'Woodrow Wilson, Jan Smuts and the Versailles Settlement', *American Historical Review* (July 1961).

J. B. DUROSELLE, 'General de Gaulle's Europe and Jean Monnet's Europe', *The World Today* (January 1966).

R. EMERSON, 'Colonialism, Political Development and the UN', *International Organisation* (Summer 1965).

L. M. GOODRICH, 'From League of Nations to United Nations', *International Organisation* (February 1947).

E. B. HAAS, 'Technological Self-reliance for Latin America: The OAS Contribution', *International Organisation* (Autumn 1980).

E. J. HUGHES, 'Winston Churchill and the Formation of the United Nations Organisation', *Journal of Contemporary History* (October 1974).

J. M. VAN DER KROEF, 'ASEAN's Security Needs and Policies', *Pacific Affairs* (Summer 1974).

D. E. LEE, 'The Genesis of the Veto', *International Organisation* (February 1947).

C. LEGUM, 'The Organisation of African Unity: Success or Failure?', *International Affairs* (April 1975).

L. L. LEONARD, 'The United Nations and Palestine', *International Conciliation*, no. 454 (1949).

B. D. MEYERS, 'Intraregional Conflict Management by the OAU', *International Organisation* (Summer 1974).

K. J. MIDDLEBROOK, 'Regional Organisations and Andean Economic Integration 1969–1975', *Journal of Common Market Studies* (September 1978).

O. J. B. OJO, 'Nigeria and the Formation of ECOWAS', *International Organisation* (Autumn 1980).

SHEE POON-KIM, 'A Decade of ASEAN, 1967–1977', *Asian Survey* (August 1977).

R. VARGAS-HIDALGO, 'The Crisis of the Andean Pact: Lessons for Integration among Developing Countries', *Journal of Common Market Studies* (March 1979).

I. WALLERSTEIN, 'The Early Years of the OAU', *International Organisation* (Autumn 1966).

O. R. YOUNG, 'International Regimes: Problems of Concept Formation', *World Politics* (April 1978).

References

1. THE ORIGINS OF THE LEAGUE OF NATIONS

1. W. S. Churchill, *The World Crisis: The Aftermath* (London, 1929) p. 142.
2. About 200 disputes went to arbitration between 1815 and 1900.
3. P. S. Reinsch, *Public International Unions* (Boston, 1911) p. 21.
4. Ibid., p. 6 for an early use of the term 'interdependence'.
5. L. S. Woolf, *International Government* (London, 1916) pp. 102–4.
6. Ibid., p. 104.
7. *The Proceedings of the Hague Peace Conferences: The Conference of 1899*, Carnegie Endowment for International Peace (New York, 1920) pp. 18–19.
8. Ibid.
9. This was, in fact, little more than a list of arbitrators who were available to states which might wish to make use of their services.
10. F. Wilson, *The Origins of the League Covenant* (London, 1928) pp. 18, 58.
11. H. W. V. Temperley, *A History of the Peace Conference of Paris*, vol. IV, (London, 1924) p. 24.
12. Castlereagh, speaking on the proposed Protocol of the Congress of Troppau, quoted in Woolf, *International Government*, p. 24.
13. Viscount Grey, *Twenty Five Years* (New York, 1925) p. 256.
14. E. Bendiner, *A Time for Angels* (London, 1975) p. 12. See also F. P. Walters, *A History of the League of Nations* (London, 1952) p. 18.
15. D. F. Fleming, *The United States and the League of Nations, 1918–1920* (New York, 1932) pp. 3–8.
16. Ibid.
17. For a summary of the work of these groups, see A. Zimmern, *The League of Nations and the Rule of Law* (London, 1936) pp. 160–73; also A. J. Mayer, *Political Origins of the New Diplomacy, 1917–1918* (New Haven, Conn., 1959) pp. 46–155.
18. D. H. Miller, *The Drafting of the Covenant*, vol. I (New York, 1928) p. 4.
19. R. S. Baker, *Woodrow Wilson: Life and Letters* (London, 1939).
20. Bryan actually claimed that this idea originated in similar proposals that he had been advancing for some years as a means of resolving labour disputes. *The Memoirs of William Jennings Bryan* (Washington, 1925) pp. 384–85.
21. *Papers Relating to the Foreign Relations of the United States: The Paris Peace Conference (PPC)*, vol. I (Washington, 1943) p. 23.
22. The fourteenth point stated that 'a general association of nations must be formed under specific covenants for the purpose of affording mutual guarantees of political independence and territorial integrity to great and small states alike'.
23. C. Seymour (ed.), *The Intimate Papers of Colonel House*, vol. I (London, 1928) p. 209.
24. *PPC*, vol. I, pp. 22–5.
25. R. S. Baker and W. E. Dodd (eds), *The Public Papers of Woodrow Wilson*, vol. II (New York, 1927) pp. 184–8.

26.   *PPC*, vol. I, p. 53.
27.   Fleming, *The US and the League*, p. 12.
28.   R. Lansing, *The Peace Negotiations: A Personal Narrative* (Boston, Mass., 1921) p. 34.
29.   See his letter to House, dated 22 March 1918 in Baker, *Life and Letters*, vol. VIII, p. 43.
30.   See House's letter to Wilson, 14 July 1918, ibid., p. 279.
31.   Ibid., p. 43, also p. 74. See also S. F. Beamis (ed.), *The American Secretaries of State and their Diplomacy*, vol. X (New York, 1954) p. 154.
32.   Baker, *Life and Letters*, vol. VIII, pp. 340, 343.
33.   Baker and Dodd (eds), *Public Papers*, vol. 1, p. 330.
34.   See his exposition of the League to the Senate Foreign Relations Committee, ibid.
35.   Seymour (ed.), *Intimate Papers*, vol. IV (1928) p. 292.
36.   Ibid., p. 161.
37.   Zimmern, *The League of Nations*, pp. 196–208 for the full text of this memorandum. See also G. W. Egerton, *Great Britain and the Creation of the League of Nations* (London, 1979) pp. 94–7.
38.   Seymour (ed.), *Intimate Papers*, vol. IV, p. 292.
39.   Miller, *Drafting of the Covenant*, vol. II, p. 28. See also G. Curry, 'Woodrow Wilson, Jan Smuts and the Versailles Settlement', *American Historical Review*, vol. LXVI, no. 4 (July 1961) 968–86.
40.   *PPC*, vol. III, (1928) p. 766.
41.   Egerton, *Great Britain*, p. 114.
42.   This is in fact too great a claim for any individual, if only because many important items in the Covenant were only arrived at in the course of the actual Paris negotiations.
43.   Egerton, *Great Britain*, p. 83.
44.   Beamis (ed.), *American Secretaries of State*, vol. X, p. 154.
45.   Letter from Lansing to House, 8 April 1918, in *Papers Relating to the Foreign Relations of the United States: The Lansing Papers; 1914–1920* (Washington, 1940) pp. 118–20.
46.   Lansing, *Peace Negotiations*, pp. 48–76.
47.   Miller, *Drafting of the Covenant*, vol. II, pp. 7–15.
48.   Hankey to Balfour, 25 May 1916, cited in Egerton, *Great Britain*, p. 35.
49.   *Drafting of the Covenant*, vol. II, p. 56.
50.   Ibid., pp. 106–16.
51.   See Zimmern, *The League of Nations*, pp. 151–9.
52.   See D. Mitrany, *The Functional Theory of Politics* (London, 1975), and the same author's seminal essay, *A Working Peace System: An Argument for the Functional Development of International Organisation* (London, 1943).
53.   J. C. Smuts, 'A Practical Suggestion', in Miller, *Drafting of the Covenant*, vol. II, pp. 24–5.
54.   Seymour (ed.), *Intimate Papers*, vol. IV, p. 296.
55.   For the Italian draft see Miller, *Drafting of the Covenant*, vol. II, pp. 246–55.
56.   Ibid., p. 300.
57.   Seymour (ed.), *Intimate Papers*, vol. IV, p. 477.
58.   *PPC*, vol. II, pp. 662–3.
59.   Egerton, *Great Britain*, p. 85.
60.   See Zimmern, *The League of Nations*, p. 207, and also Lloyd George's 'Fontainbleau Memorandum' in his *Memoirs of the Peace Conference* (New Haven, 1938) p. 269.

61. A. J. Mayer, *Politics and Diplomacy of Peacemaking* (London, 1968) pp. 9, 36 and 363. See also N. G. Levin, *Woodrow Wilson and World Politics* (New York, 1968) p. 6, and J. M. Thompson, *Russia, Bolshevism and the Versailles Peace* (New York, 1966) pp. 314, 385.

62. Egerton, *Great Britain*, p. 112.

63. Ibid., p. 120.

64. Miller, *Drafting of the Covenant*, vol. I, p. 63.

65. This was Wilson's so-called 'fourth draft'.

66. Egerton, *Great Britain*, pp. 121–5.

67. Miller, *Drafting of the Covenant*, vol. II, p. 237.

68. Ibid., vol. I, pp. 168–70, vol. II, p. 264.

69. Ibid., vol. II, p. 169.

70. Wilson, *Origins of the League Covenant*, p. 93.

71. Articles 11–17 in the Covenant.

72. Article 19 in the Hurst–Miller draft. Miller, *Drafting of the Covenant*, vol. II, p. 237.

73. Telegram to Lansing from American Ambassador in Tokyo, 15 November 1918, *PPC*, vol. I, p. 490.

74. Fleming, *The US and the League*, p. 184.

75. Miller, *Drafting of the Covenant*, vol. I, pp. 286–9 for the text of the memorandum.

76. Ibid., vol. II, pp. 580–91.

77. Wilson, *Origins of the League Covenant*, pp. 64–5.

78. Harold Nicholson writes of the atmosphere in Paris following the 'sinking of the vessel of Wilsonism' as follows: 'It was almost with a panic rush that we made for the boats, and when we reached them we found our colleagues of the Italian delegation already comfortably installed. They made us very welcome.' *Peacemaking 1919* (London, 1934) p. 70.

2. THE LEAGUE OF NATIONS

1. Cf. W. S. Schiffer, *The Legal Community of Mankind* (Columbia, 1954) pp. 199 and 205.

2. I. L. Claude, *Power and International Relations* (New York, 1962) pp. 196–7.

3. F. H. Hinsley, *Power and the Pursuit of Peace* (Cambridge, 1967) pp. 307–22.

4. A. Zimmern, *The League of Nations and the Rule of Law* (London, 1936) pp. 304–5.

5. 'Report to the 2nd Assembly of the League on the Work of the Council and on the Measures Taken to Execute the Decisions of the 1st Assembly', *League of Nations Document A.9.* (1921) p. 30.

6. 'Report to the 5th Assembly', *League of Nations Document A.8.* (1924) p. 18.

7. *Documents on British Foreign Policy (DBFP)* 1st ser. vol. XIII (London, 1963) p. 489.

8. Ibid., vol. VII (1958) pp. 134–5.

9. *DBFP*, ser. 1A, vol. I (London, 1966) p. 847.

10. Ibid., p. 848.

11. B. Dexter, *The Years of Opportunity: The League of Nations, 1920–1926* (New York, 1967) pp. 171–6.

12. *DBFP*, ser. 1A, vol. I, p. 7.

13. Notes of a conversation between Lloyd George and Briand, 5 January 1922, *DBFP*, vol. XIX (1974) p. 13.

14. *DBFP*, vol. XI (1961) pp. 337, 355—6, 372—3.

15. *League of Nations Document A. 37* (1920) p. 25.

16. For the text of Lloyd George's telegram to the League Secretary-General, see T. P. Conwell-Evans, *The League Council in Action* (London, 1929) p. 43.

17. 'Report to the 3rd Assembly', *League of Nations Document A. 7* (1922) p. 31.

18. *League of Nations Official Journal* (*LNOJ*) (February 1925) p. 146.

19. For a comprehensive account of this affair see J. Barros, *The Corfu Incident of 1923: Mussolini and the League of Nations* (Princeton, N.J., 1965).

20. 'Report to the 5th Assembly', *League of Nations Document A. 8.* (1924) p. 19.

21. 'Report to the 7th Assembly', *League of Nations Document A. 6* (1926).

22. Cited in E. Bendiner, *A Time for Angels* (London, 1975) p. 218.

23. Dexter, *The Years of Opportunity*, p. 135.

24. J. Barros, *Office without Power: Secretary-General Sir Eric Drummond, 1919—1933* (Oxford, 1979) p. 252.

25. Ibid., p. 253—7.

26. See J. Barros, *Betrayal from Within: Joseph Avenol, Secretary-General of the League of Nations, 1933—1940* (New York, 1969) pp. 47—51 and Bendiner, *A Time for Angels*, pp. 317—19, Zimmern, *The League of Nations*, pp. 424—30.

27. The United States did however join a separate 'mediatory group', Zimmern, *The League of Nations*, p. 429.

28. The most comprehensive study of the Manchurian crisis is C. Thorne, *The Limits of Foreign Policy: The West, the League and the Far Eastern Crisis of 1931—1933* (London, 1972).

29. Japan's reasons for withdrawing from the League included an assertion of the 'just and equitable principle' that it was necessary for the operation of the Covenant to vary in accordance with the actual conditions prevailing in different regions of the world, *LNOJ* (May 1933) p. 657.

30. For one example out of many of this kind of thinking in the British Foreign Office, see *DBFP*, ser. 2, vol. VIII, pp. 681—82.

31. See F. P. Walters, *A History of the League of Nations*, vol. II (London, 1952) p. 474.

32. *DBFP*, ser. 2, vol. VIII, pp. 679—80.

33. Ibid., pp. 714—15.

34. For example, when China made a new appeal in January 1932, invoking Articles 10 and 15 for the first time, Japan insisted that this meant that the Chinese needed to supply the Council with a freshly documented statement of their case. 6th meeting of the Council, *LNOJ* (January 1932) pp. 339—42.

35. Fifth meeting of the Council (28 January 1932) *LNOJ* (January 1932) pp. 327—8.

36. Telegram from the Tokyo Embassy, *DBFP*, ser. 2, vol. VIII, p. 700.

37. 'Foreign Office Memorandum', ibid., pp. 826—9.

38. For the text of the Ethiopian appeal, see *LNOJ* (May 1935).

39. Telegram to the French Ambassador in Rome, 19 July 1935, cited in G. Warner, *Pierre Laval and the Eclipse of France* (London, 1968) p. 96.

40. Laval had gone some way towards implying as much during a visit to Rome in January 1935, while another important indication came at the Stresa Conference of April 1935 between France, Britain and Italy, whose final communiqué opposed the unilateral repudiation of treaties but restricted this to

cases which might endanger the peace 'of Europe'. See E. M. Robertson, *Mussolini as Empire Builder: Europe and Africa, 1923–1936* (London, 1977) pp. 114–16 and 129–31.

41.   J. Barros maintains that part of the responsibility for the League's non-involvement in the early stages of the Ethiopian crisis rested with the Secretary-General, Avenol, whose consistent advice was that the affair should be settled informally between the major powers. This may be crediting him with rather more influence than he in fact possessed. See *Betrayal from Within*.

42.   Warner, *Pierre Laval*, p. 106 and Robertson, *Mussolini*, pp. 172–3.

43.   See *DBFP*, 2nd ser. vol. XV, *passim*, for details of these differences.

44.   'Minute by Sir R. Vansittart on the Position of Sanctions and the Possibility of Closing the Suez Canal to Italian Shipping', *DBFP*, 2nd ser. vol. XVI, pp. 358–60.

45.   Memorandum dated 27 November 1935 by Sir S. Hoare and Mr A. Eden on a possible oil embargo, in *DBFP*, 2nd ser. vol. XV, pp. 332–40.

46.   Telegram to British Ambassador in Washington, 4 December 1935, *DBFP*, 2nd ser., vol. XV, p. 377.

47.   Hoare and Eden Memorandum, *DBFP*, 2nd ser., vol. XV, pp. 332–40.

48.   See for example, telegram dated 26 November 1935 from Sir S. Hoare to the British Ambassador in Washington, *DBFP*, 2nd ser., vol. XV, pp. 324–5.

49.   Memorandum dated 15 December 1935 from the British Ambassador in Paris to Sir S. Hoare, *DBFP*, 2nd ser., vol. XV, pp. 480–2.

50.   Ibid.

51.   *LNOJ* (June 1936).

52.   For details of the Convention, see *LNOJ* (1930) Special Supplement no. 84.

53.   *LNOJ* (January 1936) pp. 24–6.

54.   *DBFP*, 2nd ser., vol. XV, pp. 269 and 274–5.

55.   Robertson, *Mussolini*, p. 185.

56.   *LNOJ* (June 1936) p. 660.

57.   The problem of the 'sources' of international law is a controversial one. However, the dominant approach is probably the 'positivist' one, which argues that only treaties and the established customs of states create binding obligations.

58.   M. O. Hudson, *The Permanent Court of International Justice, 1920–1942* (New York, 1943) pp. 92–112.

59.   Article 9 of the Statute of the Court.

60.   Sir Hersch Lauterpacht, *The Development of International Law by the International Court* (London, 1958) pp. 273–6.

61.   Ibid., p. 4, and S. Rosenne, *The World Court* (New York, 1973) p. 25.

62.   R. P. Dhakali, *The Codification of Public International Law* (Manchester, 1970) p. 115.

63.   S. Rosenne (ed.), *The League of Nations Committee for the Progressive Codification of International Law (1925–1928)*, vol. I (Oceana Publications, 1972) introduction, pp. xxx–xxxi.

64.   See ibid. for the history of this committee.

65.   Sir Hersch Lauterpacht, however, disagrees with this verdict: *The Development of International Law*, p. 7.

66.   The American Council on Public Affairs, *World Organisation* (Washington, 1942) p. 265.

67.   Bendiner, *A Time for Angels*, pp. 328–32.

68.   American Council on Public Affairs, *World Organisation*, p. 250.

69.   *LNOJ* (February 1936) p. 203.

70.   For further details on the regulations for each type of mandate, see the

152 THE RISE OF THE INTERNATIONAL ORGANISATION

League of Nations, *The Mandates System* (Geneva, 1945) pp. 24–32; F. White, *Mandates* (London, 1926) pp. 24–30, and Q. Wright, *Mandates under the League of Nations* (Chicago, 1930) pp. 24–63.

71. In its first report the Commission declared: 'We shall endeavour to exercise our authority less as a judge from whom critical pronouncements are expected than as collaborators who are resolved to devote their experience and their energies to a joint endeavour.' Cited in Wright, *Mandates*, p. 196.

72. *The Bruce Report on the Technical Work of the League*, Special Supplement to the Monthly Summary of the League of Nations (September 1939) p. 7.

73. Report to the 4th Assembly, *League of Nations Document A.10* (1923) pp. 49–59.

74. Supplementary Report to the 8th Assembly, *League of Nations Document A.13 (a)* (1927) pp. 21–31.

75. League of Nations Secretariat, *Ten Years of World Co-operation* (Geneva, 1930) pp. 199–201.

76. Walters, *History of the League of Nations*, vol. II, pp. 518–23.

77. *LNOJ* (January 1932) pp. 152–4.

78. American Council on Public Affairs, *World Organisation*, p. 173.

79. See *The Bruce Report*, and League of Nations Secretariat, *Ten Years of World Co-operation*, pp. 232–60.

80. Report to the 2nd Assembly, *League of Nations Document A.9.* (1921) p. 64.

81. M. Burton, *The Assembly of the League of Nations* (New York, 1974) p. 45.

82. Ibid., pp. 73–5.

83. Ibid., pp. 175–205.

84. H. Butler, *The Lost Peace* (London, 1941) p. 31.

85. Burton, *The Assembly*, p. 382.

86. Barros, *Betrayal from Within*, p. 12.

87. Barros, *Office without Power*, p. 395.

88. Ibid., p. 291.

89. Ibid., p. 54.

3. THE UNITED NATIONS IN WORLD POLITICS

1. This is made quite explicit in some of the earlier British position papers on the UN. See, for example, the memorandum by the British Foreign Secretary, Anthony Eden, on a future world organisation in which he says: '(i) It is improbable that the League of Nations can be revived in its old form but it is highly desirable that some international machinery, embodying many of the good features of the League, should be established on the conclusion of hostilities. (ii) In any case every effort should be made to preserve those technical and humanitarian services of the League which have been so conspicuously successful in the past.' Text of memorandum in P. A. Reynolds and E. J. Hughes, *The Historian as Diplomat* (London, 1976) Appendix B, pp. 126–34.

2. E. J. Hughes, 'Winston Churchill and the Formation of the United Nations Organisation', *Journal of Contemporary History*, vol. 9., no. 4. (October 1974) pp 177–94; Cordell Hull, *The Memoirs of Cordell Hull*, vol. II (New York, 1948) pp. 1640–46.

3. D. Yergin, *The Shattered Peace* (London, 1978) pp. 47–8. See also T. M. Campbell, *Masquerade Peace: America's UN Policy, 1944–45*, (Tallahassee, 1973) pp. 1, 89, 147, 156–7.

4. Reynolds and Hughes, *The Historian as Diplomat*, p. 129.

5. G. L. Goodwin, *Britain and the United Nations* (London, 1957) p. 17.

6. Campbell, *Masquerade Peace*, p. 37, and United States Department of State, *Foreign Relations of the United States* (FRUS) (Washington, 1946) vol. I, p. 127.

7. A. Z. Rubinstein and G. Ginsburgs, *Soviet and American Policies in the United Nations* (New York, 1971) p. 3.

8. Hull, *Memoirs*, vol. II, p. 1682. See also Stalin's speech of 6 November 1944, *International Conciliation* (December 1944) p. 814.

9. Campbell, *Masquerade Peace*, pp. 36—7.

10. Hull, *Memoirs*, vol. II, p. 1648.

11. L. D. Weiler and A. P. Simons, *The United States and the United Nations* (New York, 1967) p. 40.

12. For Truman's own account see *The Memoirs of Harry S. Truman*, vol. I (London, 1955) pp. 193, 201, 210—11.

13. Hull, *Memoirs*, pp. 1625—7; Weiler and Simons, *The US and the UN*, pp. 17—18.

14. The Yalta formula was written into the Charter as Article 27. See also D. E. Lee, 'The Genesis of the Veto', *International Organisation* (February 1947) 33—42.

15. Hull, *Memoirs*, pp. 1706—7. See also note 6, this page, *FRUS*, vol. I (1946) pp. 544—711.

16. United Nations Information Organisation, *Documents of the United Nations Conference on International Organisation (UNCIO)*, vol. I (1945) p. 125.

17. Ibid.

18. Ibid., pp. 173—8.

19. For a detailed comparison of the Covenant and Charter, see L. M. Goodrich, 'From League of Nations to United Nations', *International Organisation*, vol. I (1947), and H. G. Nicholas, *The United Nations as a Political Institution* (London, 1975) pp. 14—40.

20. L. M. Goodrich and E. Hambro, *Charter of the United Nations, Commentary and Documents* (London, 1949) pp. 110—21.

21. The Security Council's decisions were to be binding upon the whole membership of the UN. See a briefing given to the US delegation to the UN, *FRUS*, vol. I (1946) p. 129.

22. Ibid., pp. 1136—7.

23. Ibid., pp. 1167—71.

24. Ibid., pp. 142, 149, 153—6, 166—9.

25. For an account of the debate, see Trygve Lie, *In the Cause of Peace* (New York, 1954) pp. 31—3.

26. Weiler and Simons, *The US and the UN*, p. 125.

27. Trygve Lie, *In the Cause of Peace*, pp. 81—8.

28. Goodwin, *Britain and the UN*, pp. 74—8.

29. Ibid., pp. 113—14.

30. Weiler and Simons, *The US and the UN*, pp. 203—7.

31. B. V. Cohen, 'The Impact of the United Nations on United States Foreign Policy', *International Organisation*, vol. 5, no. 2 (May 1951) p. 277.

32. *FRUS*, vol. II (1950) p. 31.

33. For detailed discussion of the UN's work in relation to decolonisation, see M. El-Ayouty, *The United Nations and Decolonisation* (The Hague, 1971); R. Emerson, 'Colonialism, Political Development and the UN', *International Organisation*, vol. 19, no. 3 (Summer 1965); H. K. Jacobson, 'The United Nations and Colonialism: A Tentative Appraisal', *International Organisation*, vol. 16, no. 1 (Winter 1962).

34. For an account of the UN's handling of the Palestine question during

1947—9, see L. L. Leonard, 'The United Nations and Palestine', *International Conciliation*, no. 454 (1949) 603—786.

35. *UNSCOP Report to the General Assembly*, UN Document A/364 (October 1947).

36. See *FRUS*, vol. V (1947) pp. 999—1328, and vol. V (1948) *passim*; also G. T. Mazuzan, *Warren R. Austin at the UN, 1946—1953* (Kent State University Press, 1977) pp. 94—115.

37. *FRUS*, vol. V (1947) pp. 1177—8.

38. Ibid., pp. 1281—2.

39. See, for example, *Report by the Policy Planning Staff on the Position of the United States with Respect to Palestine* (19 January 1948), in *FRUS*, vol. 5, Part 2 (1948) pp. 546—54, the criticisms of this by Dean Rusk, then Director of the Office of Special Affairs (renamed the Office of United Nations Affairs on 28 January 1948) in a memorandum dated 26 January 1948, ibid., pp. 556—62, and the reply by Kennan to this, on 29 January, ibid., pp. 573—80.

40. See, for example, message to the President, 21 February 1948, ibid., pp. 637—40, and Truman's reply, ibid., p. 645.

41. Truman, *Memoirs*, vol. II, (1956) p. 157.

42. *FRUS*, vol. 5 (1948) p. 657.

43. Ibid., pp. 690—6. Cf Truman's explanation of his Palestine policy: 'the matter had been placed in the hands of the United Nations, and, *true to my conviction that the United Nations had to be made to work*, I had confidence that a solution would be found there'. *Memoirs*, vol. II, p. 157. Emphasis added.

44. J. L. Gaddis, 'Korea in American Politics, Strategy and Diplomacy, 1945—50', in Yonosuke Nagai and Akira Iruyo (eds), *The Origins of the Cold War in Asia* (University of Tokyo Press, 1977) pp. 282—3.

45. The USSR had been absent from the Security Council since January 1950 in protest against the continued seating of the Nationalist Chinese represetatives on China's permanent seat in the Security Council, which they believed rightfully belonged to the Chinese Communists.

46. For Truman's response to the North Korean attack, see his *Memoirs*, vol. 2, p. 333, and *FRUS*, vol. VII (1950) pp. 160 and 183. For Bradley's comment see ibid., p. 158.

47. See memorandum by the Director of the Office of North-east Asian Affairs, 24 July 1950, ibid., pp. 458—61, and draft memorandum prepared in the Department of Defence, ibid., pp. 502—10.

48. A. James, *The Politics of Peacekeeping* (London, 1969).

49. R. Hiscocks, *The Security Council* (London, 1973) pp. 266—8.

50. W. R. Frye, *A United Nations Peace Force* (London, 1957) pp. 10—14.

51. For a discussion of the legal controversy surrounding the creation of UNEF, see D. W. Bowett, *United Nations Forces* (London, 1964), esp. pp. 93—103.

52. Hammarskjöld, quoted in Frye, *UN Peace Force*, p. 15.

53. U Thant, *View from the UN* (London, 1977) p. 223.

54. Ibid., p. 227.

55. James, *Politics of Peacekeeping*, p. 205.

56. There is substantial literature on the Congo intervention, but see especially R. Higgins, *UN Peacekeeping, 1946—67*, vol. III (London, 1980), and G. Abi-Saad, *The United Nations Operation in the Congo, 1960—64* (Oxford University Press, 1978).

57. Security Council Resolution S/4741 (21 February 1961) quoted in full in Higgins, *UN Peacekeeping*, p. 30.

58. Ibid., pp. 243—63.

59. Rubinstein and Ginsburgs, *Soviet and American Policies in the UN*, p. 150.

60. Hiscocks, *The Security Council*, pp. 204—5.

61. Higgins, *UN Peacekeeping*, pp. 396—8.

62. For details of this controversy, see ibid., pp. 274—303, and J. G. Stoessinger, *The United Nations and the Superpowers*, 3rd edn (New York, 1973) pp. 103—25.

63. M. P. Doxey, *Economic Sanctions and International Enforcement*, 2nd edn (London, 1980) p. 68.

64. Ibid., pp. 73—9, 114—19.

65. Two books which discuss the UN's functional work in its entirety are M. Elmandjra, *The United Nations System, an Analysis* (London, 1973), and M. Hill, *The United Nations System: Co-ordinating its Economic and Social Work* (Cambridge, 1978).

66. Its role in the human rights area is discussed in Chapter 6.

67. W. R. Sharp, *The United Nations Economic and Social Council* (New York, 1969) pp. 73—5.

68. Hill, *The UN System*, pp. 66—71, 105—8.

69. J. P. Sewell, *UNESCO and World Politics* (Princeton, 1975) pp. 85—103.

70. R. Hoggart, *An Idea and its Servants: UNESCO from Within* (London, 1978) p. 26.

71. Sewell, *UNESCO*, pp. 251—4.

72. Hoggart, *An Idea and its Servants*, pp. 75—81.

73. Ibid., p. 194.

74. Ibid.

75. *FRUS*, vol. II (1949) pp. 15—22.

76. Ibid., p. 17.

77. Ibid., p. 19.

78. Ibid., pp. 20—1.

79. W. F. Buckley, cited in D. P. Moynihan, *A Dangerous Place* (London, 1979) p. 29.

80. A. Yeselson and A. Gaglione, *A Dangerous Place* (New York, 1974).

81. Ibid., p. 157.

82. UN General Assembly, 30th Session, Resolution 3379, 10 November 1975.

83. Cf. D. A. Kay, *The New Nations in the United Nations, 1960—1967* (New York, 1970) p. 187.

84. Churchill, *The World Crisis*.

85. D. A. Kay, *The Changing United Nations* (New York, 1977) p. 3.

86. *FRUS*, vol. II (1950) p. 46.

87. See, for example, Trygve Lie, *In the Cause of Peace*, pp. 275—322; U Thant, *View from the UN*, pp. 20—84.

88. U Thant, *View from the UN*, p. 27.

4.   THE EUROPEAN COMMUNITY

1. For the text of Monnet's memorandum, see R. Vaughan, *Postwar Integration in Europe* (London, 1976) pp. 51—6.

2. R. C. Mowatt, *Creating the European Community* (London, 1973) p. 57.

3. Vaughan, *Post-war Integration*, pp. 94—106.

4. Ibid., pp. 16—20.

5. Churchill was actually accused by the prominent Italian federalist Altiero Spinelli of making his speech with the 'clever and cynical' aim of enabling the British to take over the leadership of the European movement, 'which they would guide so as to make sure a real union would never be achieved'. A. Spinelli, 'The Growth of the European Movement since World War II', in M. Hodges (ed.),

European Integration (London, 1972) pp. 58—9. This, however, ignores the fact that Churchill was not in power when he made this speech, which was designed to encourage union in continental Europe, of which Churchill did not feel Britain was part.

6.   Vaughan, *Postwar Integration*, p. 18.

7.   Dean Acheson, *Present at the Creation* (London, 1970), p. 341; Konrad Adenauer, *Memoirs, 1945—53* (London, 1966) pp. 199—206.

8.   M. Beloff, *The United States and the Unity of Europe* (London, 1963) p. 5.

9.   *FRUS*, vol. III (1949) p. 134.

10.   Beloff, *The US and the Unity of Europe*, p. 14. Dulles, who was later to be Secretary of State under Eisenhower, was at the time one of the Republican Party's leading spokesmen on foreign affairs and as part of the bipartisan approach to foreign policy of President Truman, he held a number of significant posts during the Truman administration.

11.   M. Palmer *et al., European Unity: A Survey of the European Organisations* (London, 1968) p. 29.

12.   Mowatt, *Creating the European Community*, pp. 38—42.

13.   *FRUS*, vol. II (1948) pp. 711—16.

14.   Acheson, *Present at the Creation*, p. 339; and *FRUS*, vol. III (1950) pp. 697—701.

15.   Ibid.

16.   *FRUS*, vol. III (1949) p. 631. See also Adenauer, *Memoirs*, pp. 200—6.

17.   See Chapter Six.

18.   Mowatt, *Creating the European Community*, p. 28.

19.   *FRUS*, vol. III (1950) pp. 646—52.

20.   Note from Bevin to Schuman, cited ibid., pp. 709—10.

21.   French reply to Bevin's note, ibid., pp. 712—14. Also 'Anglo-French Discussions Regarding French Proposals for the Western European Coal, Iron and Steel Industries', Cmd 7970 (1950).

22.   Preamble, ECSC Treaty.

23.   R. Pryce, *The Politics of the European Community* (Boston, 1973) p. 6.

24.   Ibid., p. 7.

25.   *FRUS*, vol. III (1950) pp. 167—8.

26.   Ibid., pp. 273—8.

27.   For a discussion of the allied conflict over German rearmament, see R. McGeehan, *The German Rearmament Question* (Chicago, 1971).

28.   Mowatt, *Creating the European Community*, p. 127.

29.   Ibid., pp. 128—30.

30.   Text of the Messina Resolution in Keesings Research Report, *The European Communities: Establishment and Growth* (Keesings Publications, 1975) pp. 9—12.

31.   W. Pickles, 'Political Power in the European Community', in C. A. Cosgrove and K. J. Twitchett (eds), *The New International Actors* (London, 1970) pp. 201—21.

32.   Monnet's speech on this theme in May 1962 is quoted in Mowatt, *Creating the European Community*, pp. 154—5.

33.   G. Ionescu, *The New Politics of European Integration* (London, 1972).

34.   The Commission's recommendations on speeding up the implementation of the Rome Treaty are in *The Bulletin of the European Economic Community* (*BEEC*) (March 1960) pp. 14—24.

35.   *BEEC* (May 1961) p. 7.

36.   Pryce, *Politics of the EEC*, p. 15.

37. *BEEC* (April 1961) p. 24.

38. *BEEC* (April 1960).

39. Cosgrove and Twitchett, *The New International Actors*, p. 44.

40. See Macmillan's statement to the House of Commons at the time of Britain's application, *BEEC* (September—October 1961) pp. 8—10.

41. Mowatt, *Creating the European Community*, p. 159; Beloff, *The US and the Unity of Europe*, pp. 103—20.

42. *BEEC* (September—October 1961) pp. 8—10.

43. Piers Dixon, *Double Diploma: The Life of Sir Pierson Dixon* (London, 1968) pp. 284—91.

44. Pryce, *Politics of the EEC*, p. 18.

45. Merging the Communities had first been proposed in 1959 by the Belgian Foreign Minister, Pierre Wigny. *BEEC* (April 1965) p. 11.

46. M. Camps, *European Unification in the Sixties* (New York, 1966) pp. 6—9.

47. Ibid., pp. 38—46; *BEEC* (May 1965) Supplement.

48. Camps, pp. 46—7.

49. Mowatt, *Creating the European Community*, pp. 179—82.

50. *BEEC* (April 1960) p. 11.

51. *BEEC* (April 1965) p. 7.

52. Ibid., p. 8.

53. J. B. Duroselle, 'General de Gaulle's Europe and Jean Monnet's Europe', *The World Today* (January 1966).

54. *BEEC* (October 1965) p. 3.

55. Ibid., p. 4.

56. *BEEC* (March 1966).

57. C. Sasse *et al., Decision-making in the European Community* (New York, 1977) p. 88.

58. *BEEC* (February 1969) p. 11.

59. Supplement to *BEEC* (January 1969). Interestingly, after his retirement Dr Mansholt changed his views on agricultural reform, becoming converted to the argument that, although inefficient in some respects, small farming units were preferable because they kept people in employment in a situation where alternative work might not be available and also because they caused less ecological damage. *The Common Agricultural Policy, Some New Thinking From Dr Sicco Mansholt*, pamphlet published by the Soil Association (August 1979).

60. *BEEC* (September—October 1969) p. 13.

61. *BEEC* (January 1970) pp. 11—16.

62. For a detailed account of the negotiations, see S. Z. Young, *Terms of Entry: Britain's Negotiations with the European Community, 1970—1972* (London, 1973).

63. D. Swann, *The Economics of the Common Market*, 4th edn (Harmondsworth, 1978) pp. 42—5.

64. *Programme of the Commission for 1979* (Brussels, 1979) p. 14.

65. 'The Second Enlargement of the European Community', *European Documentation Periodical* (Belgium, 1979) p. 13.

66. H. Wallace *et al.* (eds), *Policy-making in the European Communities* (London, 1977) pp. 188—91.

67. *European Community* (January 1976) pp. 6—8.

68. 'The EMS Jigsaw', *European Community* (January—February 1979) pp. 3—8.

69. R. Jackson and J. Fitzmaurice, *The European Parliament: A Guide to Direct Elections* (Harmondsworth, 1979) pp. 62—8.

70. London, 1973.
71. Ibid., pp. 48–54.
72. Ibid., pp. 68–85.

5.   REGIONAL ORGANISATION OUTSIDE EUROPE

1. G. Pope Atkins, *Latin America in the International Political System* (New York, 1977) p. 308.
2. M. Margaret Ball, *The OAS in Transition* (Duke University Press, 1969) p. 5.
3. Cited ibid., p. 10.
4. G. Connell-Smith, *The Inter-American System* (London, 1966) p. 15.
5. Pope Atkins, *Latin America*, pp. 322–5.
6. Bryce Wood, 'The Organisation of American States', in *The Yearbook of World Affairs, 1979* (London, 1979) p. 150.
7. G. Connell-Smith, 'The Organisation of American States', in A. Shlaim (ed.), *International Organisations in World Politics, Yearbook, 1975* (London, 1976) p. 201.
8. In the amended Charter of 1967, which came into force in 1970, the relevant Articles are numbered 18 to 22.
9. Cited in Connell-Smith, 'The Organisation of American States', p. 207.
10. I. L. Claude, 'The OAS, the UN and the United States', *International Conciliation* (March 1964).
11. Pope Atkins, *Latin America*, p. 332.
12. Ball, *The OAS in Transition*, pp. 471–2.
13. Ibid., pp. 479–80.
14. Pope Atkins, *Latin America*, pp. 330–1, Bryce Wood, 'Organisation of American States', pp. 157–9.
15. Bryce Wood, 'Organisation of American States', p. 155.
16. For a discussion of the work of the OAS in the field of technology transfer, see E. B. Haas, 'Technological Self-reliance for Latin America: The OAS Contribution', *International Organisation* (Autumn 1980) 541–70.
17. Bryce Wood, 'Organisation of American States', p. 153.
18. Article 1 of the revised Charter. Text in A. J. Peaslee, *International Governmental Organisation*, vol. I, part one (The Hague, 1974) pp. 1222–6.
19. See R. D. Baker, 'Latin American Economic Integration', in P. A. Tharp Jr (ed.), *Regional International Organizations Structures and Functions* (New York, 1971) pp. 239–41.
20. F. Parkinson, 'International Economic Integration in Latin America and the Caribbean', *The Yearbook of World Affairs, 1977* (London, 1977) p. 255.
21. Pope Atkins, *Latin America*, p. 288.
22. Ibid.
23. Parkinson, 'International Economic Integration', p. 248.
24. Ibid., p. 243.
25. K. J. Middlebrook, 'Regional Organisations and Andean Economic Integration, 1969–1975', *Journal of Common Market Studies*, vol. XVII, no. 1 (September 1978) 78–80.
26. E. S. Milenky, 'The Cartagena Agreement in Transition', *The Yearbook of World Affairs*, 1979 (London, 1979) p. 168.
27. Ibid.
28. Parkinson, 'International Economic Integration', p. 249.
29. R. Vargas-Hidalgo, 'The Crisis of the Andean Pact: Lessons for Integra-

tion among Developing Countries', *Journal of Common Market Studies*, vol. XVII, no. 3. (March 1979) 213—26.

30. Milenky, 'The Cartagena Agreement', p. 177.

31. I. Wallerstein, *Africa: The Politics of Unity* (New York, 1967) p. 7.

32. I. Wallerstein, 'The Early Years of the OAU', *International Organisation* (Autumn 1966) 775.

33. N. J. Padelford, 'The Organisation of African Unity', *International Organisation* (Summer 1964) 526.

34. J. Mayall, 'African Unity and the OAU: The Place of a Political Myth in African Diplomacy', *The Yearbook of World Affairs, 1973* (London, 1973) p. 120.

35. Cited in Peaslee, *International Governmental Organisation*, vol. 2 (1974) p. 1166.

36. S. Touval, 'The Organisation of African Unity and African Borders', *International Organisation* (Autumn 1967) 124.

37. M. Wolfers, *Politics in the Organization of African Unity* (London, 1976) pp. 46—8.

38. On the history of this dispute and the OAU's role see P. B. Wild, 'The Organisation of African Unity and the Algeria-Morocco Border Conflict', *International Organisation* (1966) pp. 18—36.

39. B. D. Meyers, 'Intraregional Conflict Management by the OAU', *International Organisation* (Summer 1974) 358—9.

40. Ibid., 356—7.

41. For details of the OAU's response to the Biafran crisis, see Z. Cervenka, 'The OAU and the Nigerian Civil War', in Y. El-Ayouty (ed.), *The Organisation of African Unity after Ten Years* (New York, 1976) pp. 152—73.

42. Ibid.

43. Ibid., pp. 165—6.

44. L. T. Kapungu, 'The OAU's Support for the Liberation of Southern Africa', ibid., p. 136.

45. Wolfers, *Politics in the OAU*, p. 189.

46. Kapungu, 'The OAU's Support', p. 144.

47. Ibid., pp. 138—9.

48. C. Legum, 'The Organisation of African Unity: Success or Failure?', *International Affairs* (April 1975) 216.

49. Ibid., 217.

50. For a discussion of the work of the OAU's specialised commissions, see Wolfers, *Politics in the OAU*, pp. 91—119.

51. Meyers, 'Intraregional Conflict Management by the OAU', p. 369.

52. O. J. B. Ojo, 'Nigeria and the Formation of ECOWAS', *International Organisation* (Autumn 1980) 571—604.

53. Cited in T. O. Elias, 'The Economic Community of West Africa', in *The Yearbook of World Affairs, 1978* (London, 1978) p. 103.

54. Ibid., p. 104.

55. On the history of ASA, see B. K. Gordon, *The Dimensions of Conflict in South-east Asia* (New Jersey, 1966) pp. 162—87.

56. For a discussion of the different attitudes towards regional security, see S. W. Simon, 'The ASEAN States: Obstacles to Security Cooperation', *Orbis* (Summer 1978) 415—34.

57. J. M. van der Kroef, 'ASEAN's Security Needs and Policies', *Pacific Affairs* (Summer 1974).

58. Shee Poon-Kim, 'A Decade of ASEAN, 1967—1977', *Asian Survey* (August 1977) p. 758.

59. Ibid., p. 761.
60. *Far Eastern Economic Review* (21 November 1975).
61. Ibid.
62. *Asian Recorder* (1–7 April 1976) p. 13,089.
63. *The Observer* (13 September 1981) p. 13.
64. Ibid.
65. *Far Eastern Economic Review* (18 February 1977).
66. *Far Eastern Economic Review* (19 August 1977).
67. *Asian Recorder* (10–16 December 1979).

6.   INTERNATIONAL REGIMES

1. Cf. O. R. Young, 'International Regimes: Problems of Concept Formation', *World Politics* (April 1978) 331–56.
2. See D. M. Leive, *International Regulatory Regimes* (Lexington Books, 1976) especially Introduction and vol. I, pp. 3–70.
3. For details of the proposed regime for the moon, see *UN Chronicle*, vol. XVII, no. 2 (March 1980).
4. *UN Conference on the Law of the Sea: Official Records* (UN Publications, 1958).
5. For the American position, see the 17 March 1981 statement by the new head of the US delegation to UNCLOS III, J. L. Malone, International Communications Agency, US Embassy, London, 19 March 1981.
6. B. Buzan, 'From the Fire to the Frying Pan? Innovations in Large-scale Negotiating Techniques at UNCLOS III' (Paper at the British International Studies Association Conference, 1979).
7. *The Times* (30 August 1980).
8. *Economic Implications of Seabed Mineral Development in the International Area*, Report of Secretary-General (May 1974).
9. *Third United Nations Conference on Law of Sea to Meet in New York*, United Nations Information Centre, BR/80/9 (March 1980) pp. 6–8.
10. Ibid., p. 13.
11. M. S. McDougal *et al.*, *Human Rights and World Public Order* (New Haven and London, 1980) pp. 238–46.
12. In the Preamble and Articles 1, 13, 55, 62, 68, and 76. See also F. Newman, 'Interpreting the Human Rights Clause of the UN Charter', *Human Rights Journal*, vol. V, no. 2 (1972).
13. For the text of the Covenants, see E. Luard (ed.), *The International Protection of Human Rights* (London, 1967) pp. 333–63.
14. *Human Rights, 1948–73: UN Action in the Field of Human Rights* (UN Publications, 1974) pp. 193–5.
15. General Assembly Document, A/10235 (7 October 1975) pp. 12–13.
16. Ibid., pp. 14–18, and S. Bailey 'UN Fact Finding and Human Rights Complaints', *International Affairs* (April 1972) 266.
17. See, for example, E. Zvoodgo, 'A Third World View', in D. Kommers and G. Loesher (eds), *American Foreign Policy and Human Rights* (Indiana: Notre Dame University Press, 1979) ch. 5.
18. International Commission of Jurists, *Uganda and Human Rights* (Geneva, 1977).
19. See V. Chkhikvadze, 'Human Rights and Non-interference in the Internal Affairs of States', *International Affairs*, no. 2 (Moscow, 1978).
20. For a detailed discussion of the American human rights system, see

L. J. Le Blanc *The OAS and the Promotion and Protection of Human Rights* (The Hague, 1977).

21. Ibid., pp. 116—22.

22. J. I. Dominguez *et al., Enhancing Global Human Rights* (New York, 1979) p. 174.

23. J. G. Townsend, 'A Latin American Perspective', in F. E. Dowrick (ed.), *Human Rights* (Westmead, 1979) pp. 107—24.

24. For a discussion of the Commission's procedure for examining admissibility, see F. G. Jacobs, *The European Convention on Human Rights* (Oxford, 1975) pp. 218—51.

25. On the problem of definition, see W. H. Smith, 'International Terrorism: A Political Analysis', *The Yearbook of World Affairs, 1977* (London 1977) pp. 138—41; and N. N. Kittrie, 'Reconciling the Irreconcilable: the Quest for International Agreement over Political Crime and Terrorism', *The Yearbook of World Affairs, 1978* (London. 1978) pp. 208—36.

26. N. D. Joyner, *Aerial Hijacking as an International Crime* (New York, 1974) pp. 131—4.

27. By 1977, 87 states were bound by the Tokyo Convention, 80 by the Hague Convention and 73 by the Montreal Convention. A. E. Evans and J. F. Murphy, *Legal Aspects of International Terrorism* (Lexington, 1978) p. 20.

28. For a recent discussion of Western European co-operation against terrorism, see J. Lodge (ed.), *Terrorism: A Challenge to the State* (Oxford, 1981) especially pp. 164—217.

29. Evans and Murphy, *Legal Aspects of International Terrorism*, p. 30.

30. *The Times* (18 July 1978) p. 1.

31. P. Wilkinson, *Terrorism and the Liberal State* (London, 1977) pp. 222—3.

32. I have benefited in writing this section from several discussions with Professor D. R. Wightman of Birmingham University's School of International Studies.

33. C. B. Gwin, 'The Seventh Special Session: Toward a New Phase of Relations between the Developed and the Developing States', in K. P. Sauvant and H. Hasenpflug (eds), *The New International Economic Order* (London, 1977) p. 98.

34. L. Anell and B. Nygren, *The Developing Countries and World Economic Order* (London, 1980) p. 88.

35. Ibid., pp. 187—91 for text of Declaration.

36. For the text of this 'Dakar Declaration', see G. F. Erb and V. Kallab (eds), *Beyond Dependency* (New York, 1975) pp. 213—28.

37. For details, see E. Lazlo *et al., The Objectives of the New International Economic Order*, UNITAR publication (New York, 1978) pp. 45—65.

38. J. E. Spero, *The Politics of International Economic Relations* (London, 1977) esp. pp. 21—61.

39. C. F. Bergsten, 'Access to Supplies and the New International Economic Order', in J. N. Bhagwati (ed.), *The New International Economic Order: The North—South Debate* (Cambridge, Mass., 1977) esp. pp. 199—203.

40. E. Lazlo *et al., The Obstacles to the New International Economic Order*, UNITAR publication (New York, 1980) pp. 41—2.

41. Ibid.

42. Sauvant and Hasenpflug (eds), *The NIEO*, p. 76.

43. For a discussion of this and other objections to the NIEO, see C. Ries, 'The "New International Economic Order": The Skeptic's View', in Sauvant and Hasenpflug (eds), *The NIEO*, ch. 4.

44. E. Rothschild, 'Food Politics', *Foreign Affairs* (January 1976).

45. *The Guardian* (15 September 1981) p. 18.

Index

164